Fave Art -16 (Funny and Sexy)

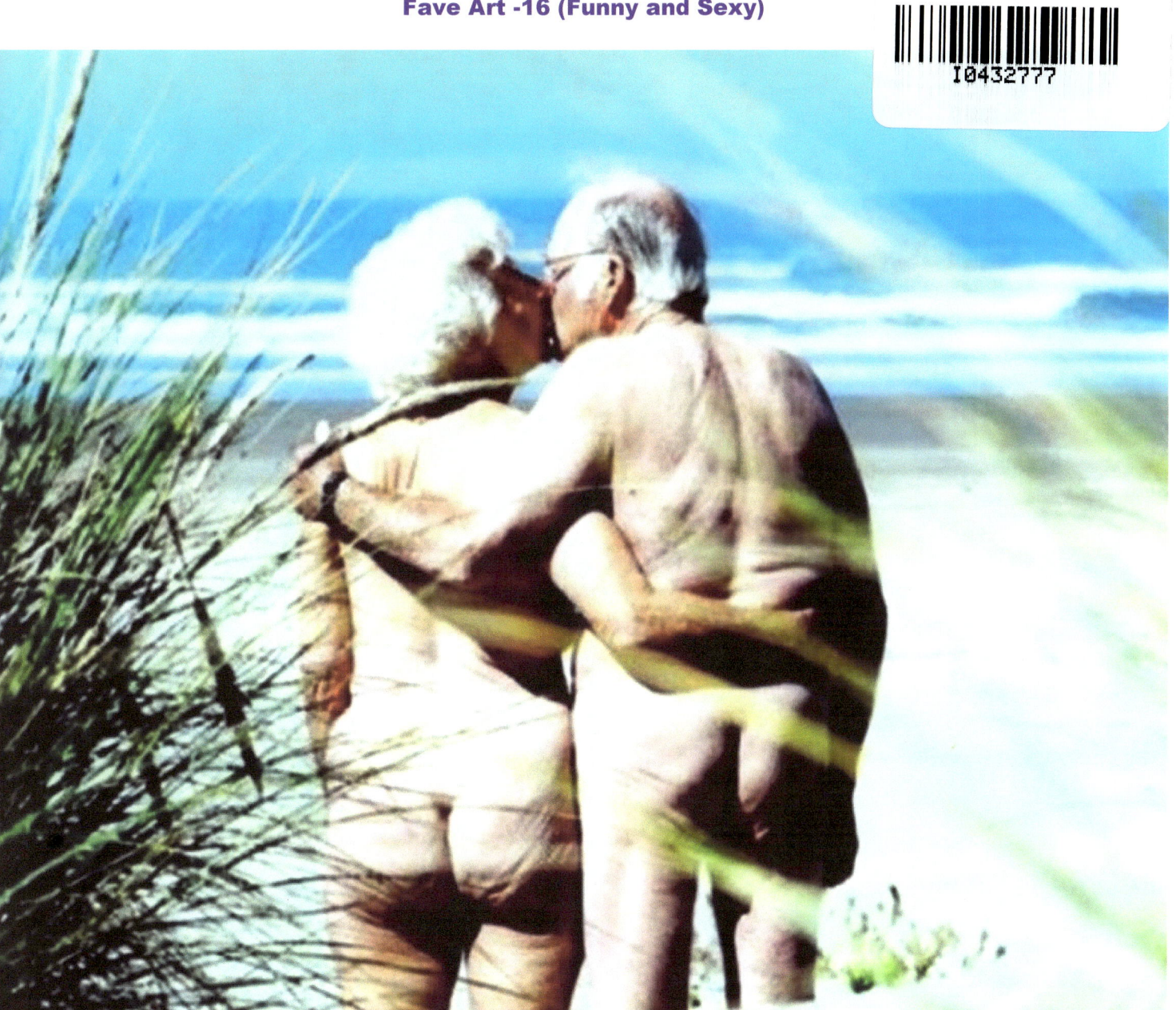

Love Never Ends, Funny & Sexy!

WELCOME! We hope you will enjoy this Fave Art-16 photo album of my favorite random collection of art and pics. Photos are copied from the internet, posters, calendars, cards and art books. You may display this book as coffee table book in your living room, as conversation piece. You may give this as gift. You may cut out each page, 8.5x11 inches, for framing. Printed by Tatay Jobo Elizes under following ISBN Code Numbers:

ISBN-13: 978- 1973838869 & ISBN-10: 1973838869

Printed in USA, 2017. Free to copy by anybody. Why copy? Just obtain the book.

Contact: job_elizes@yahoo.com (Tatay Jobo Elizes, Self-Publisher)

http://tinyurl.com/mj76ccq & http://www.jobelizes6.wix.com/mysite.

Fave Art -16 (Funny and Sexy)

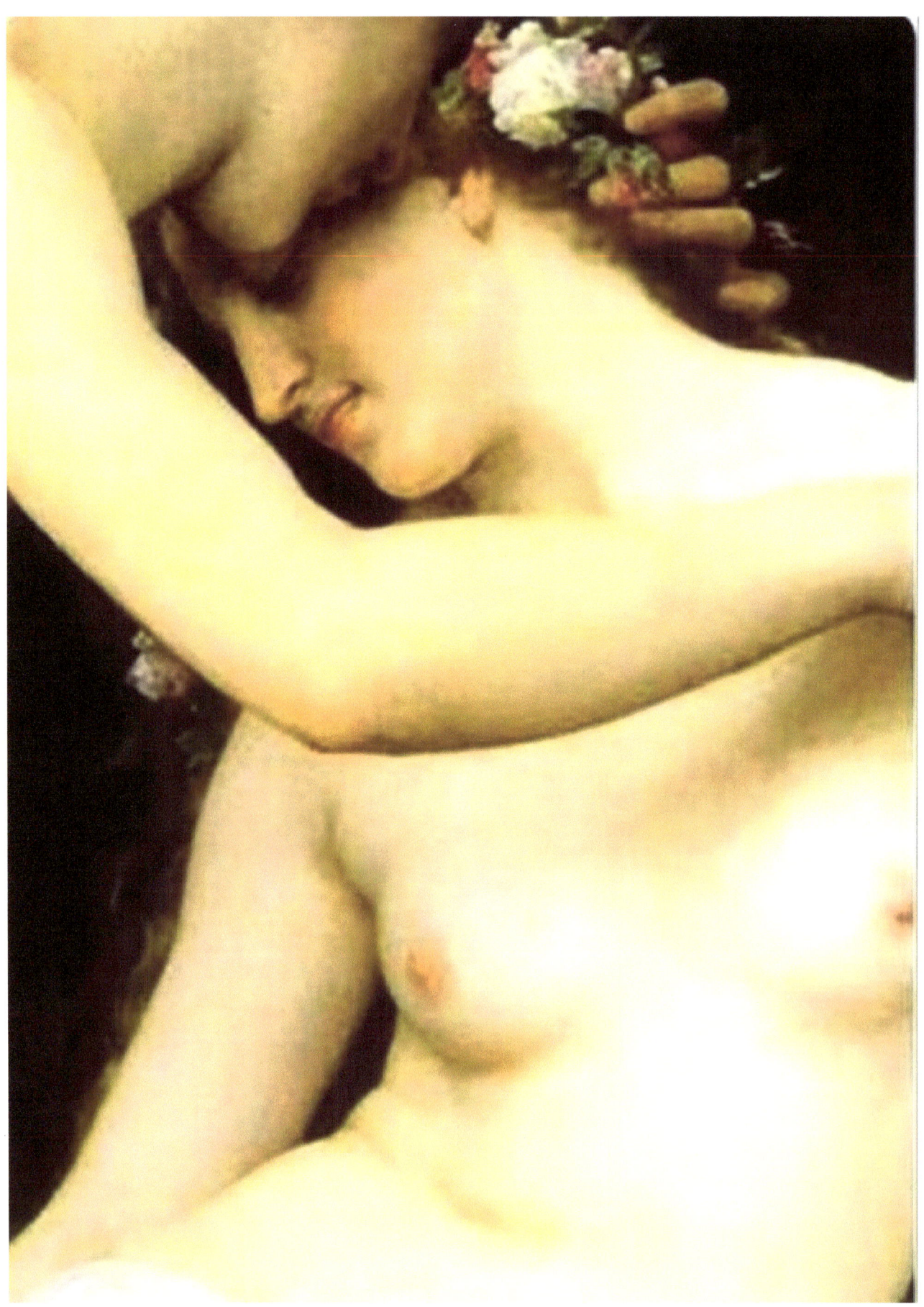

Flora and Zephyr, 1875, detail by William-Adolphe Bouguereau

Fave Art -16 (Funny and Sexy)

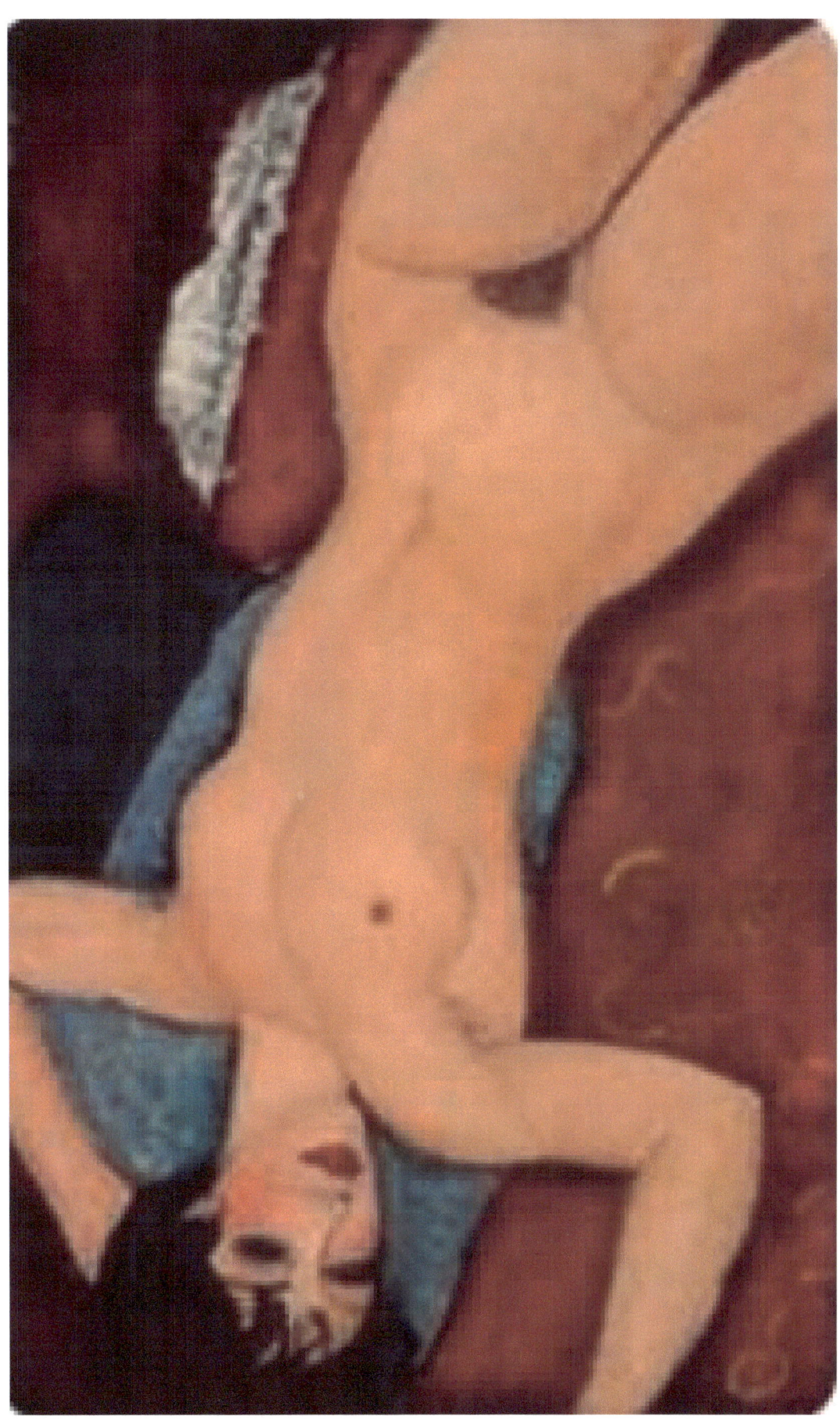

Nu Couche (Nude) by Modigliani, sold for Pounds 113,000.-

Fave Art -16 (Funny and Sexy)

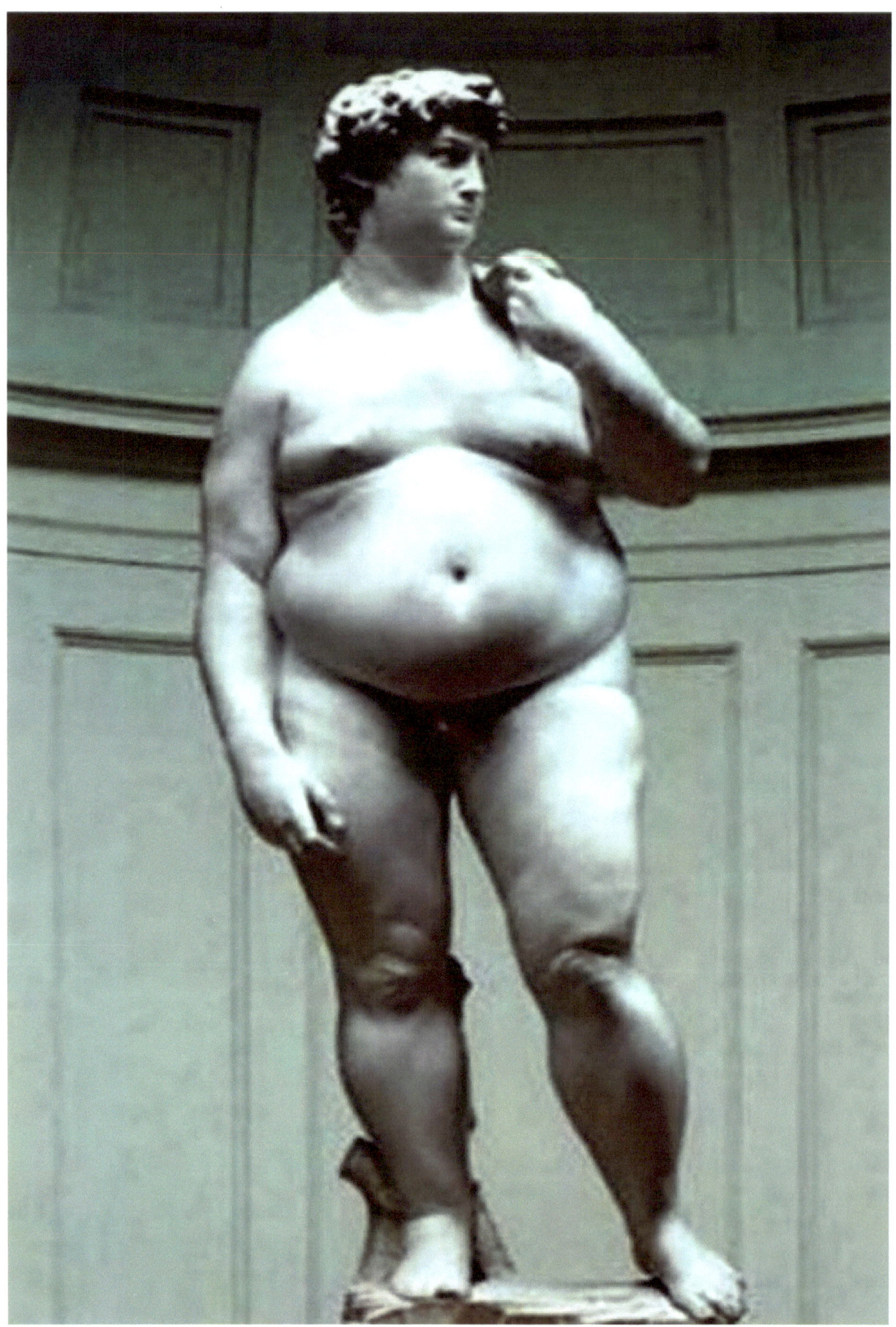

Roman Sculpture of Eros or Cupid, fattened for fun

Fave Art -16 (Funny and Sexy)

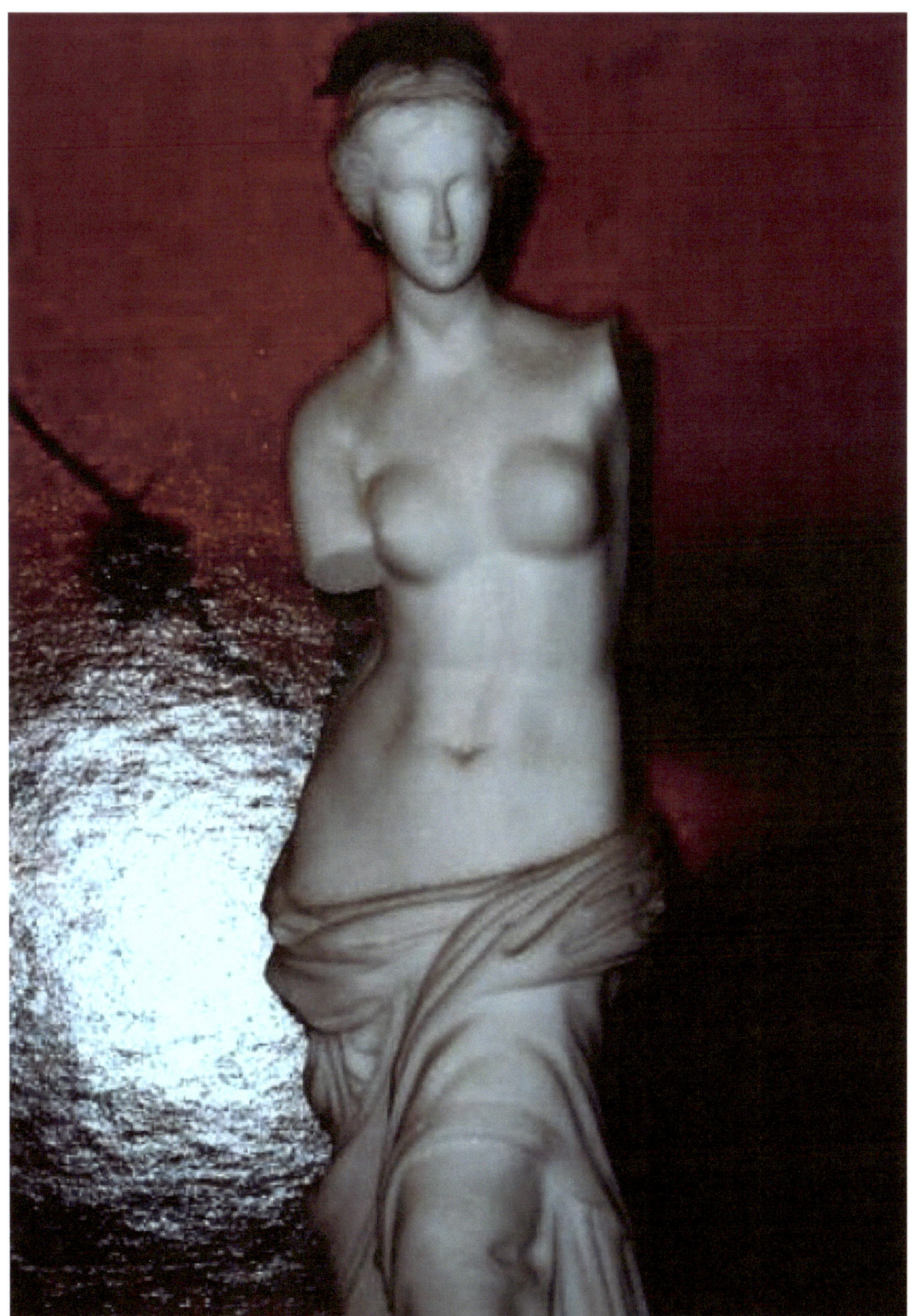

Roman Sculpture of Venus

Fave Art -16 (Funny and Sexy)

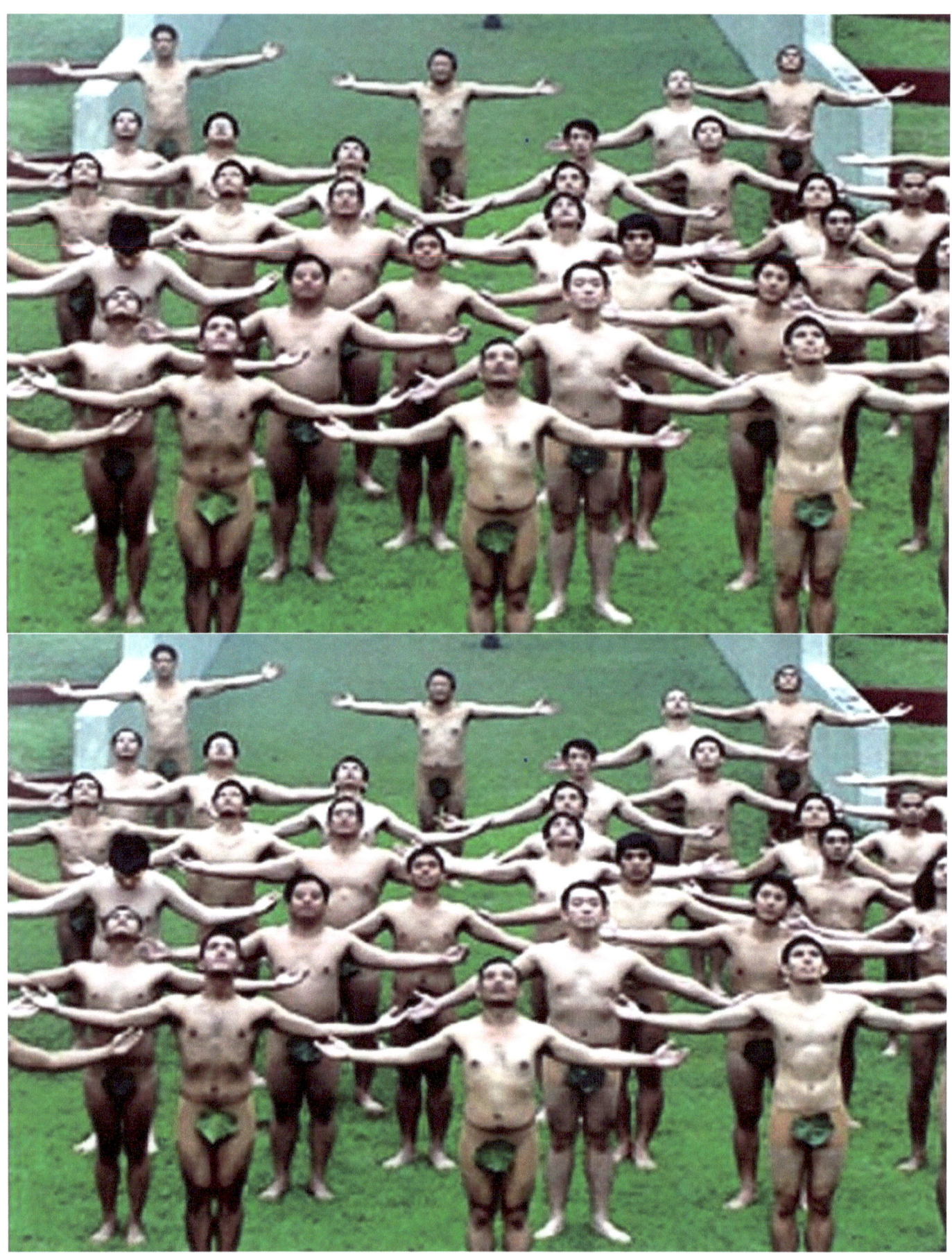

"Oblation" Parade at University of the Philippines, fun and frolic

Fave Art -16 (Funny and Sexy)

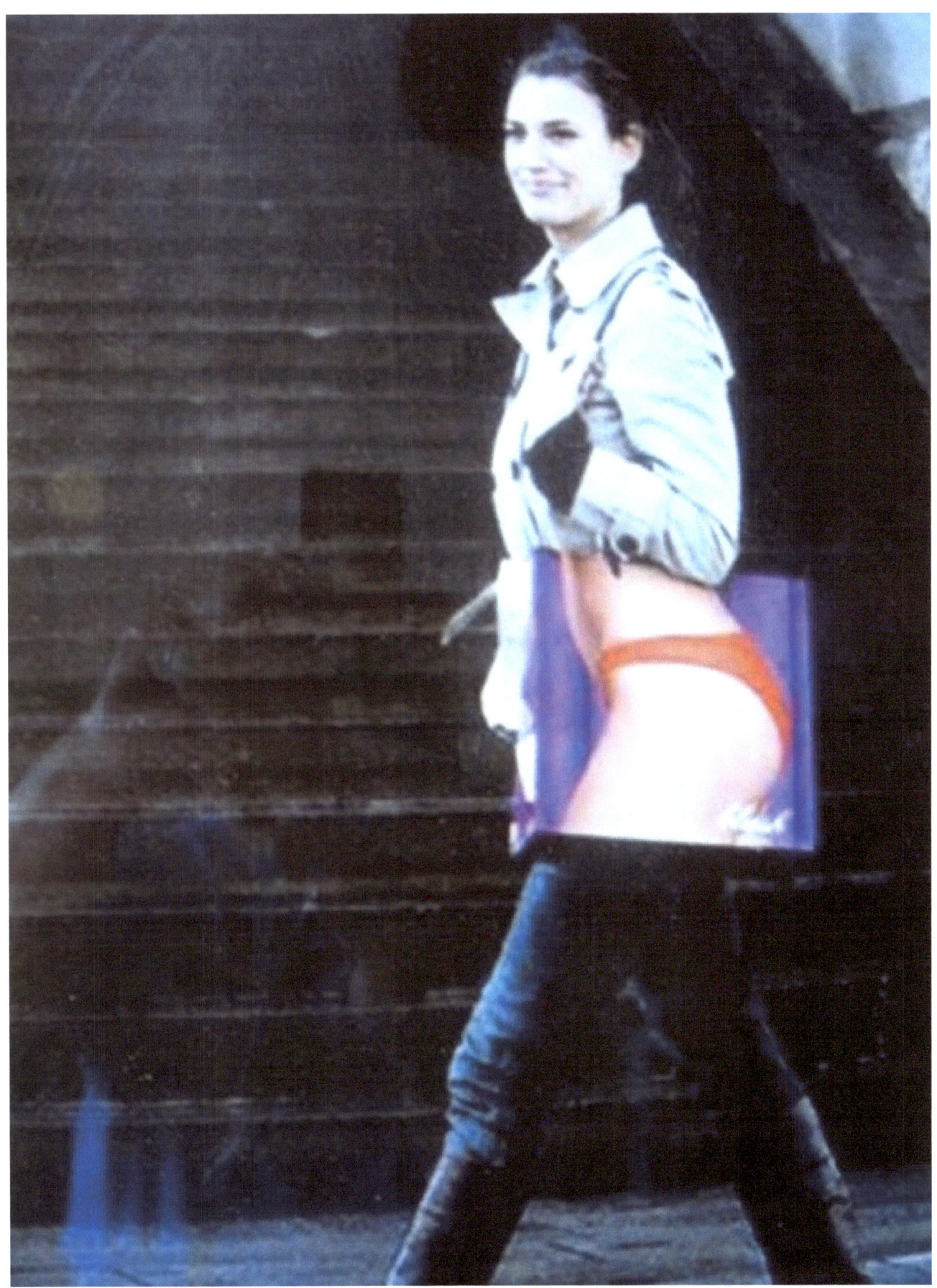

Deceptive Handbag, nice pic!

Fave Art -16 (Funny and Sexy)

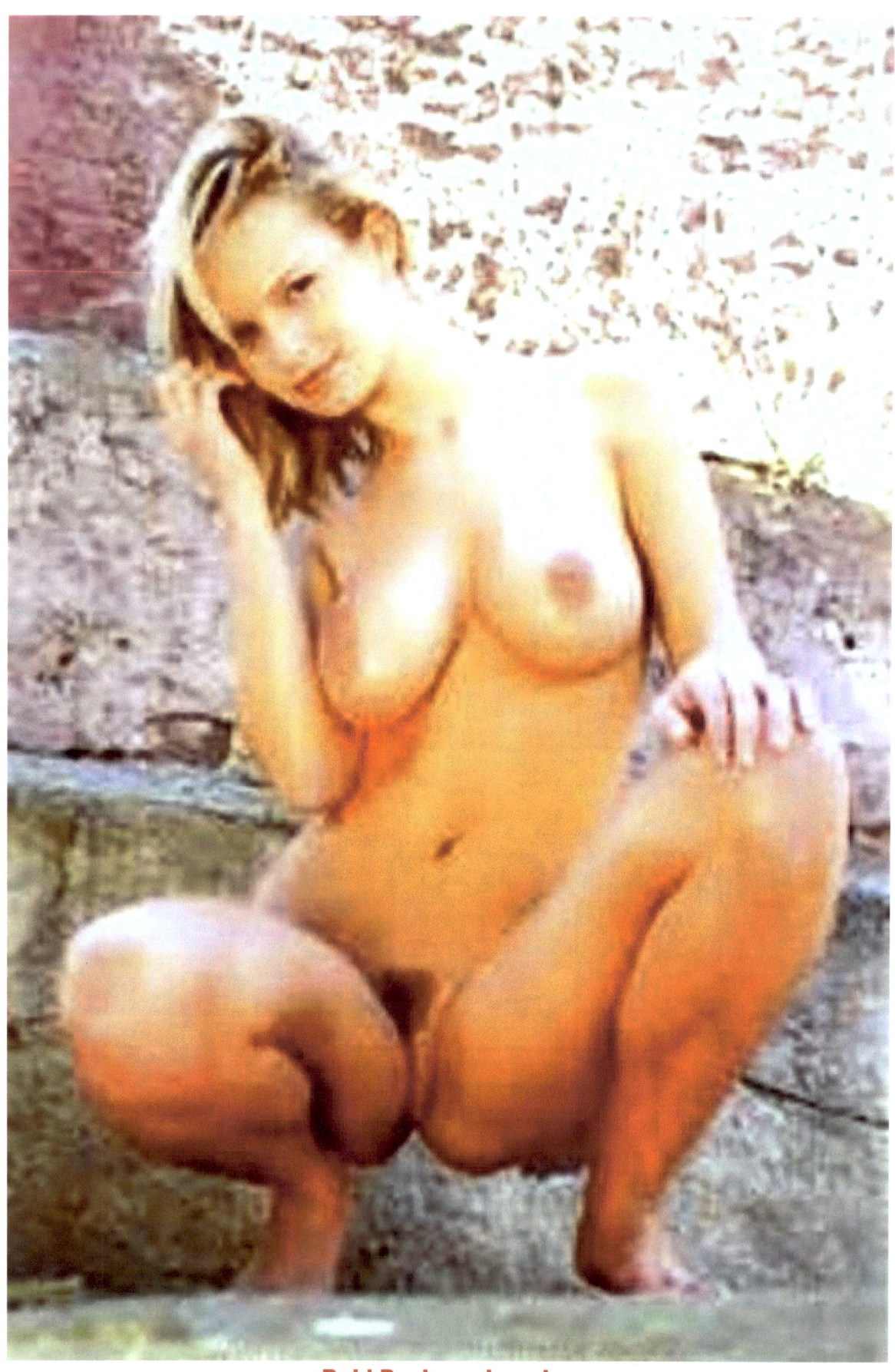

Bold Posing, nice pic.

Fave Art -16 (Funny and Sexy)

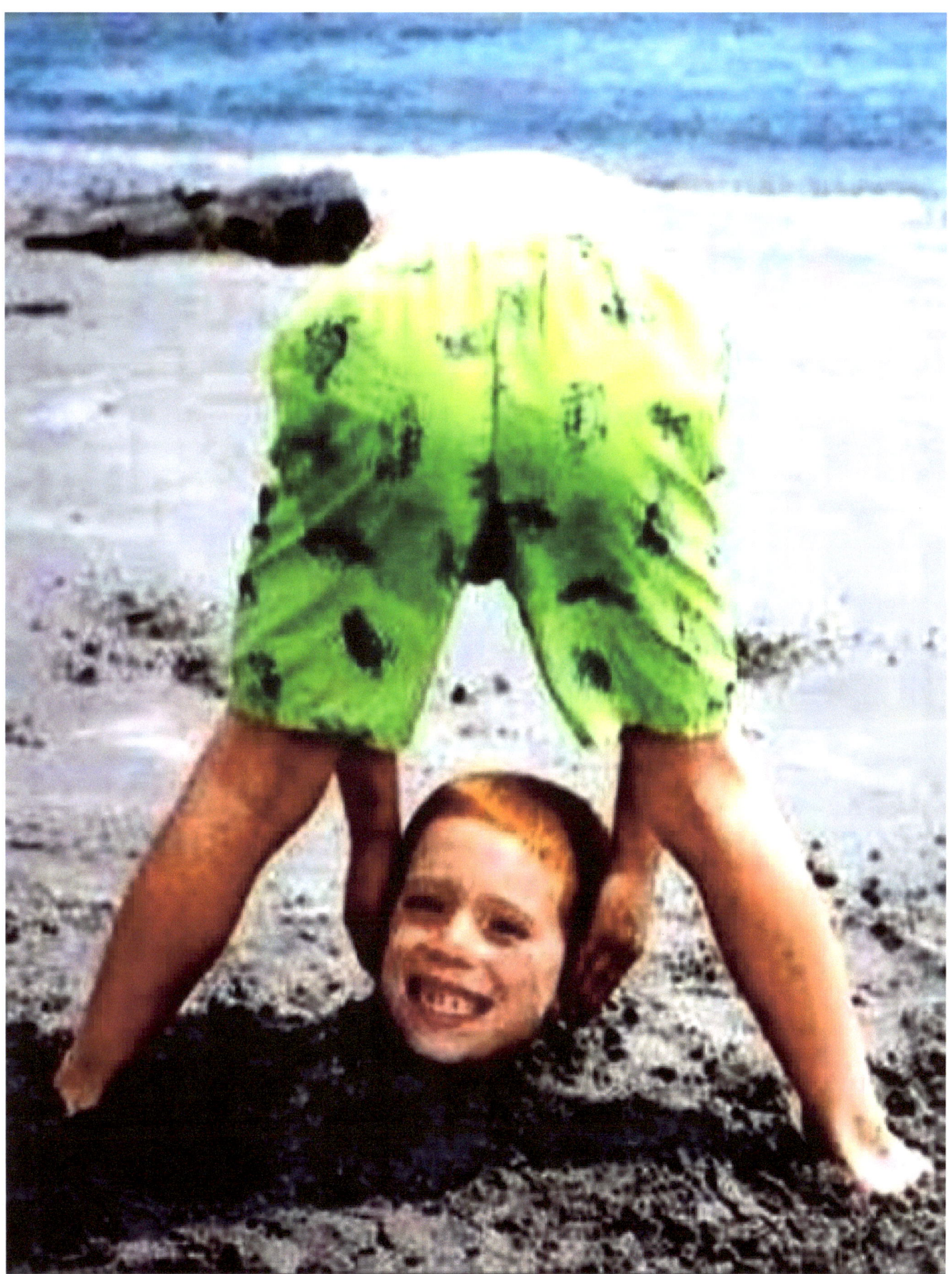

Tricky Boy, nice pic!

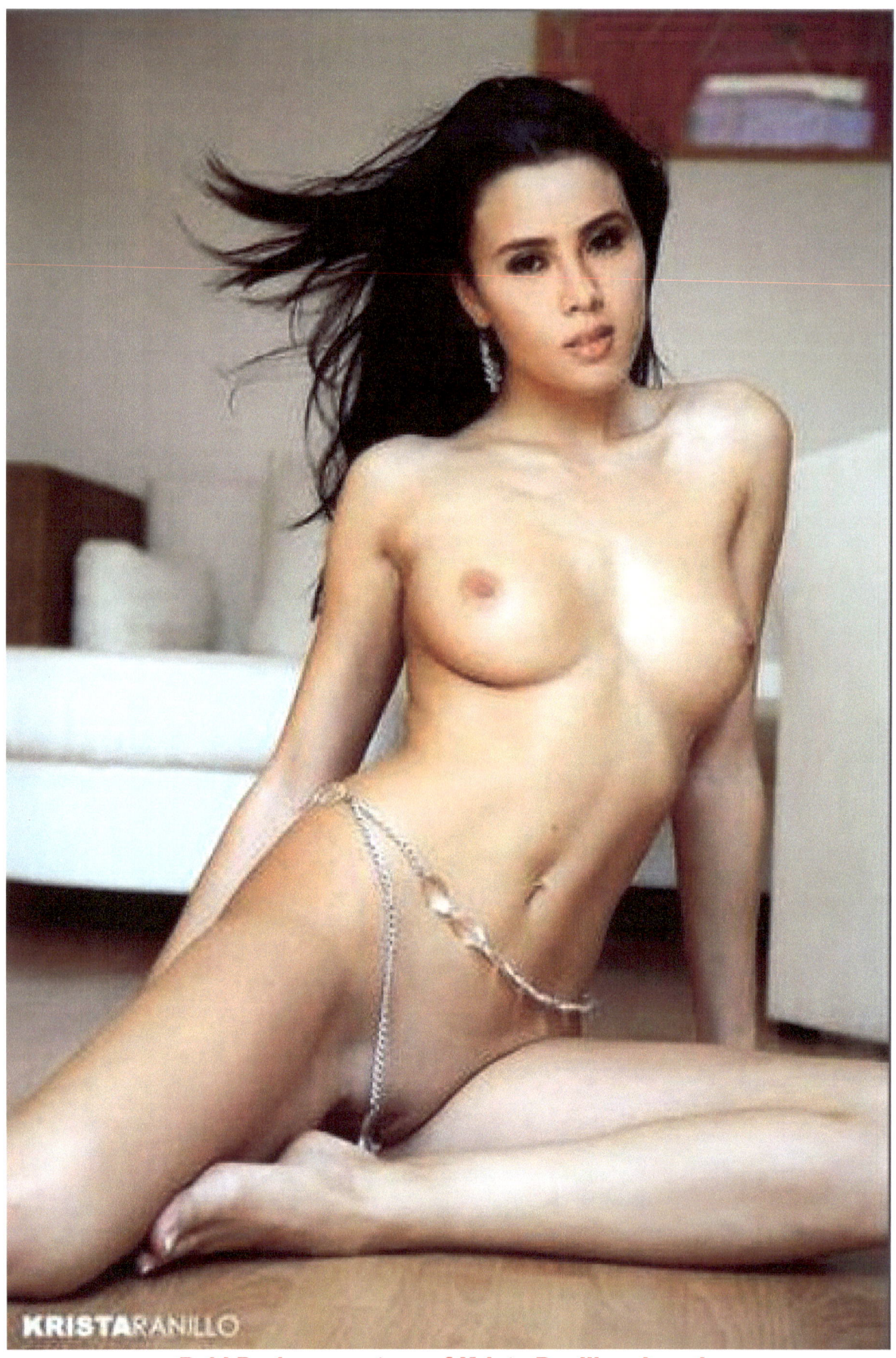

Fave Art -16 (Funny and Sexy)

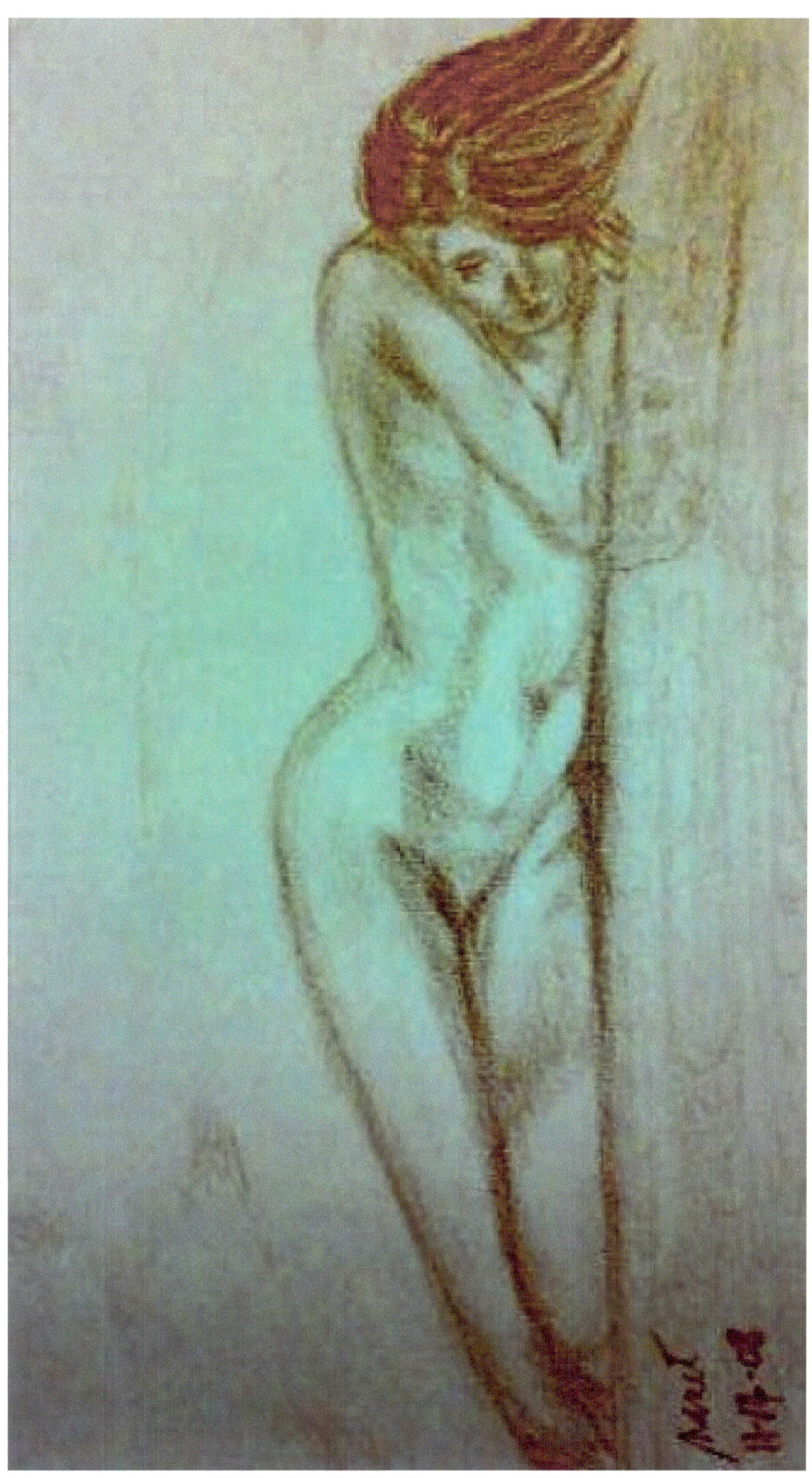

Nude Study by Nanet, my friend

Fave Art -16 (Funny and Sexy)

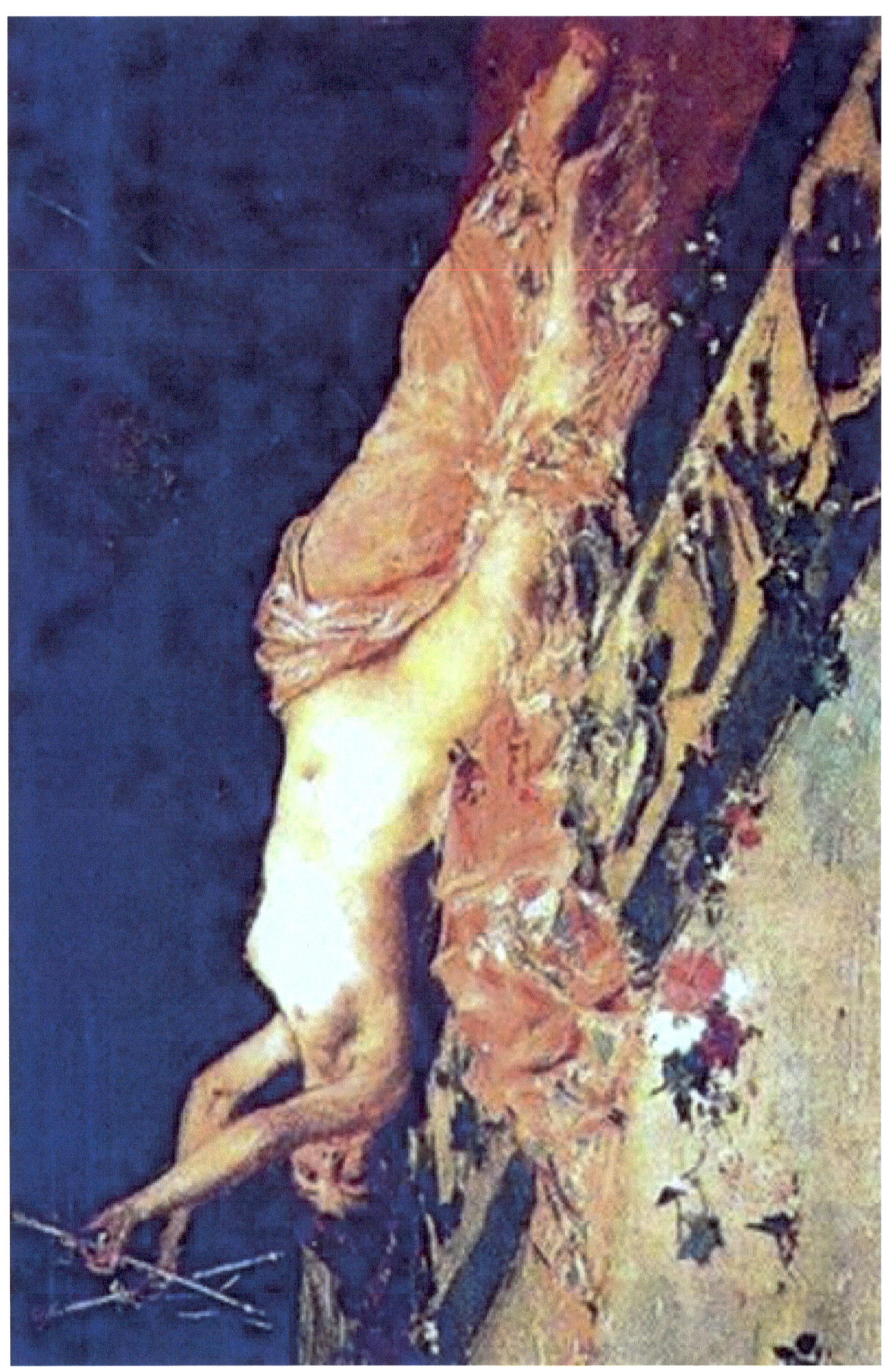

Painter/year unknown

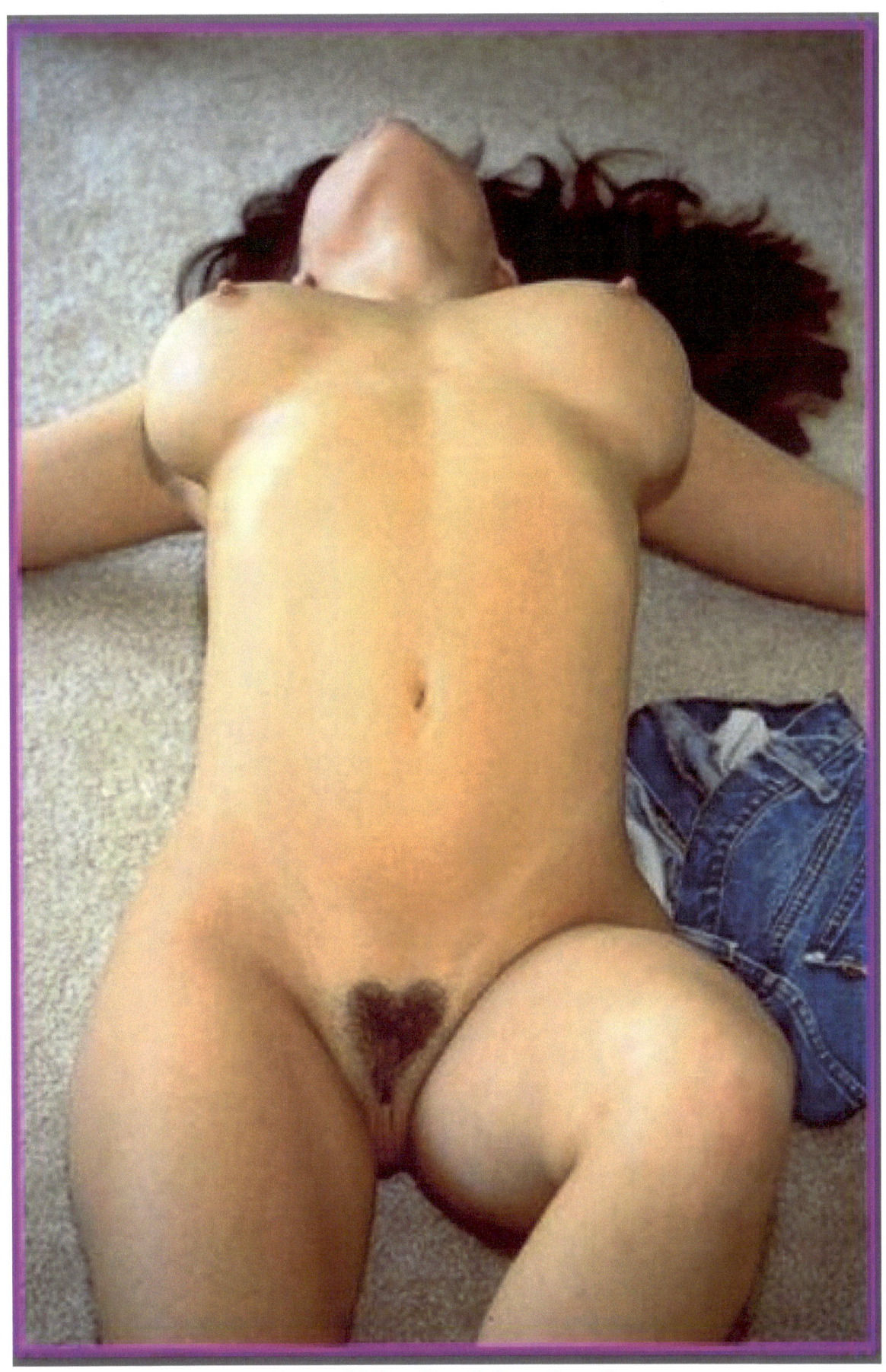

Fave Art -16 (Funny and Sexy)

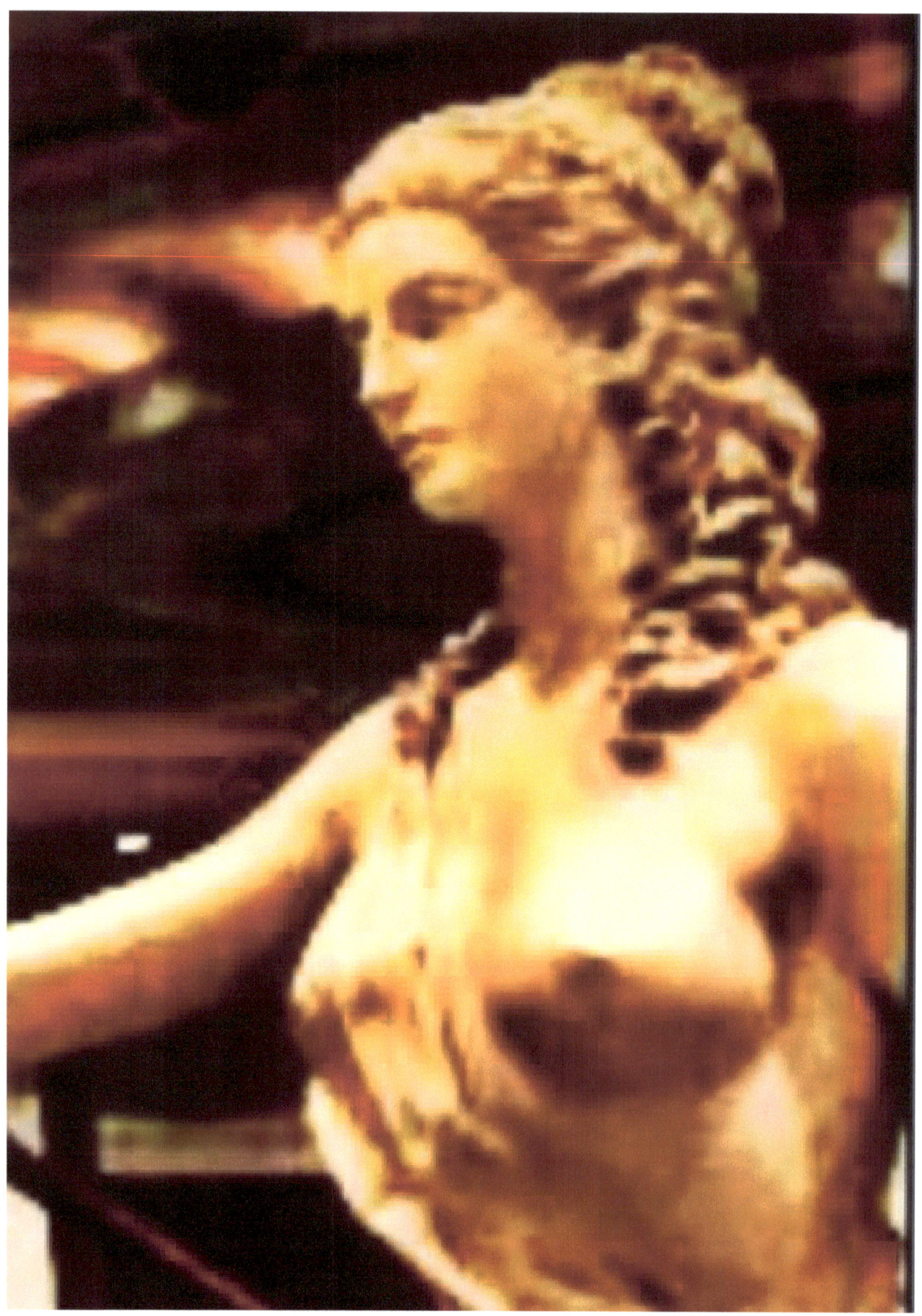

Sculpture seen in a casino, Las Vegas

Fave Art -16 (Funny and Sexy)

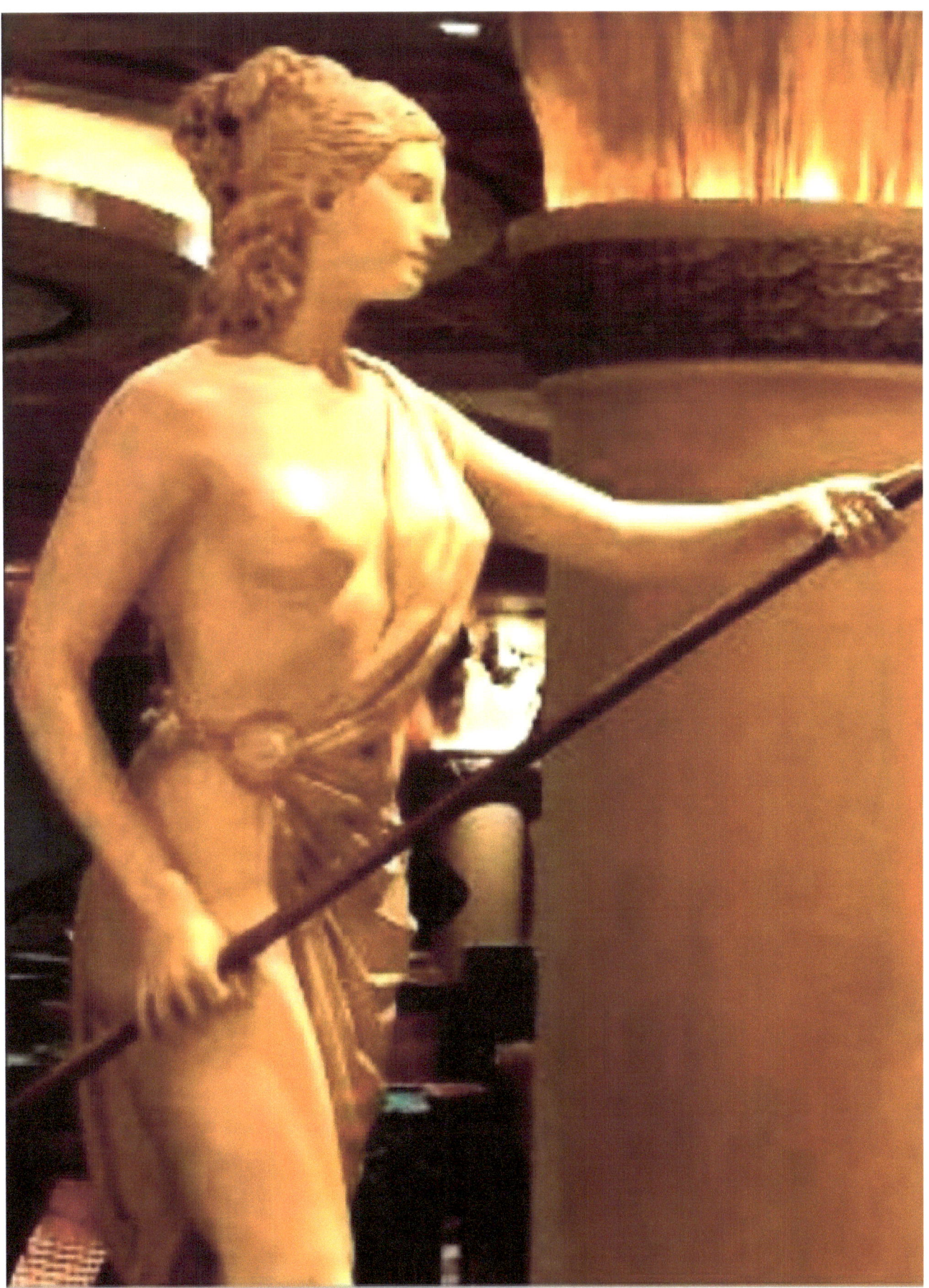

Sculpture see in a casino, Las Vegas

Fave Art -16 (Funny and Sexy)

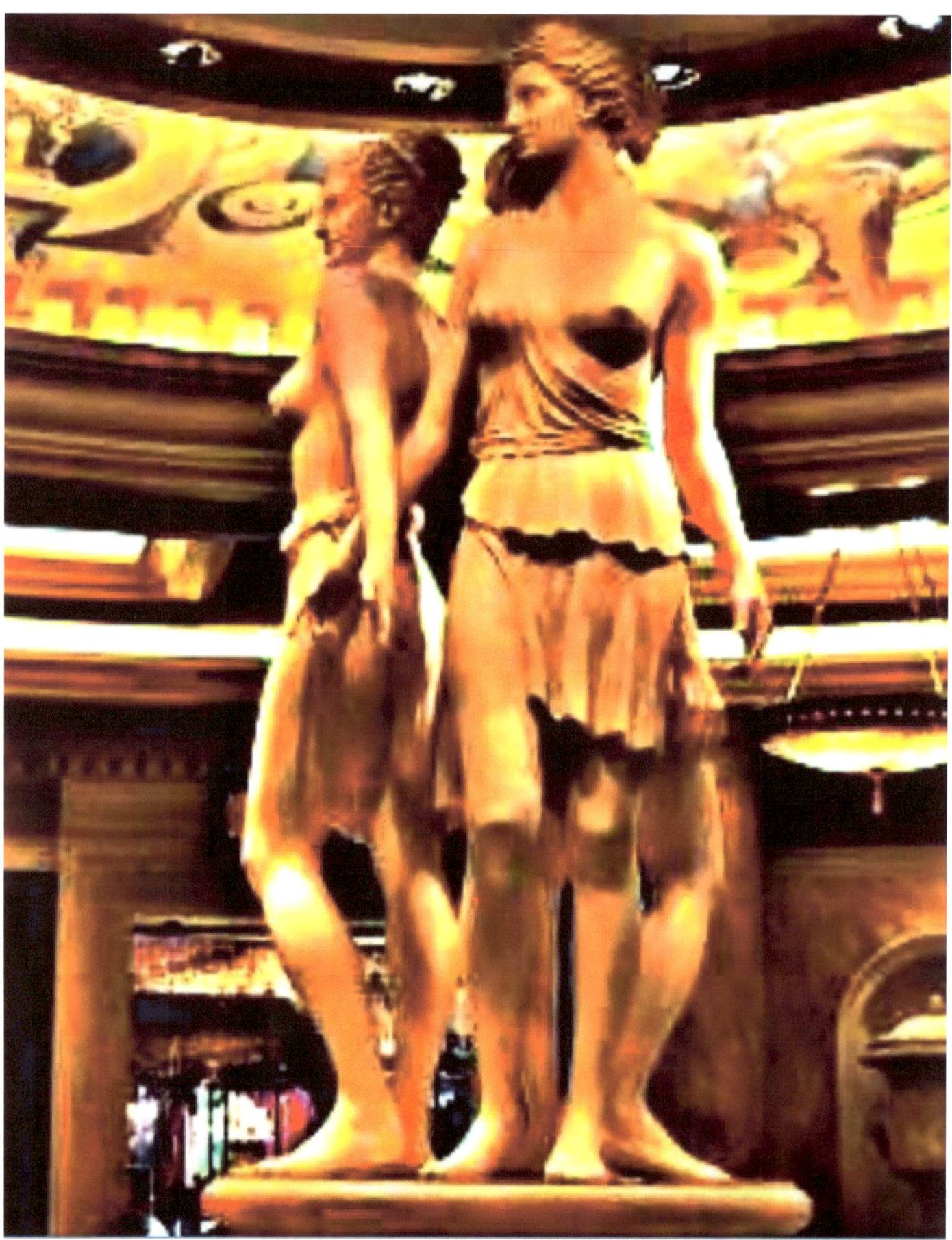

Sculpture see in a casino in Las Vegas

Fave Art -16 (Funny and Sexy)

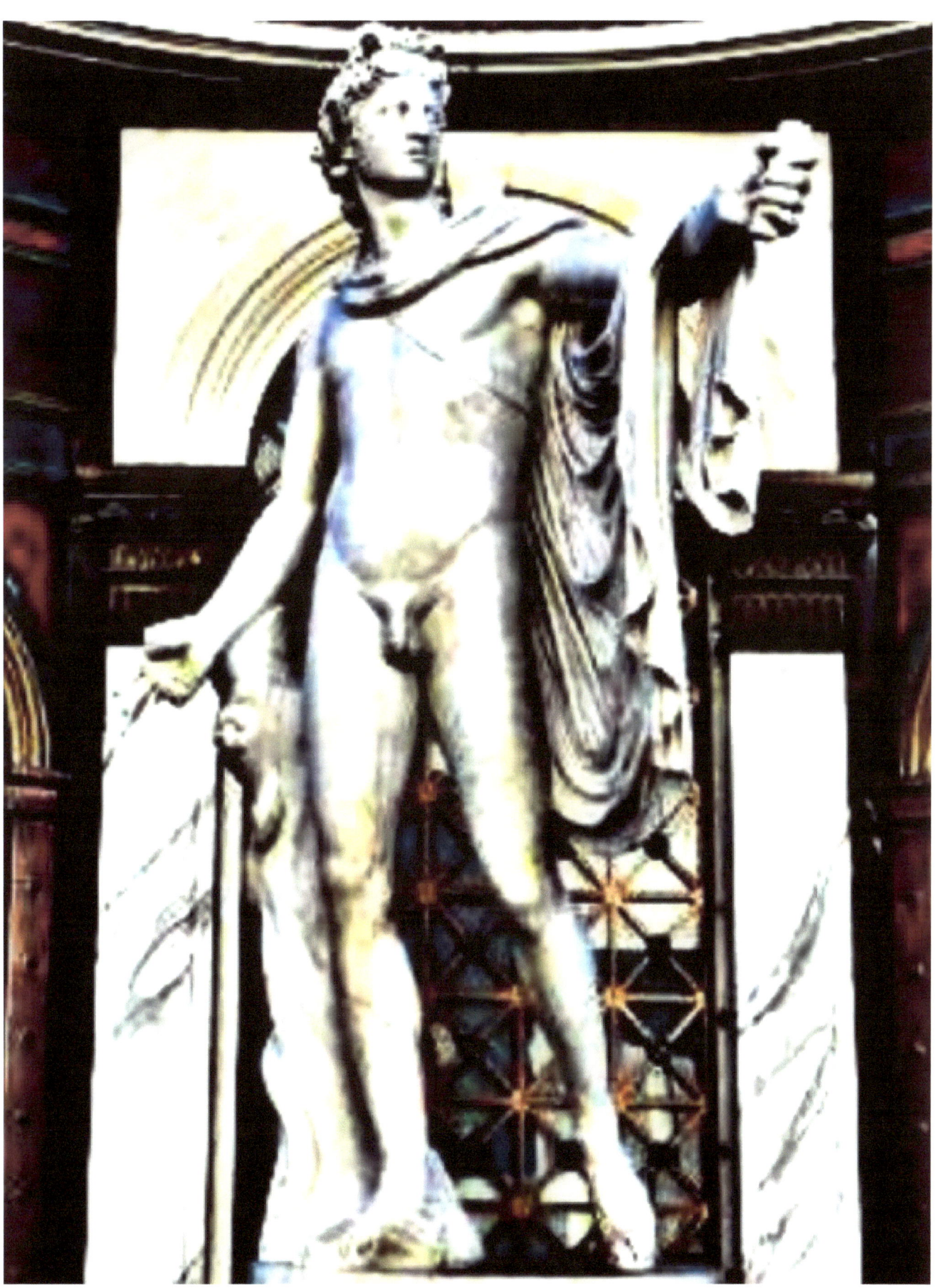

A normal Roman sculpture

Fave Art -16 (Funny and Sexy)

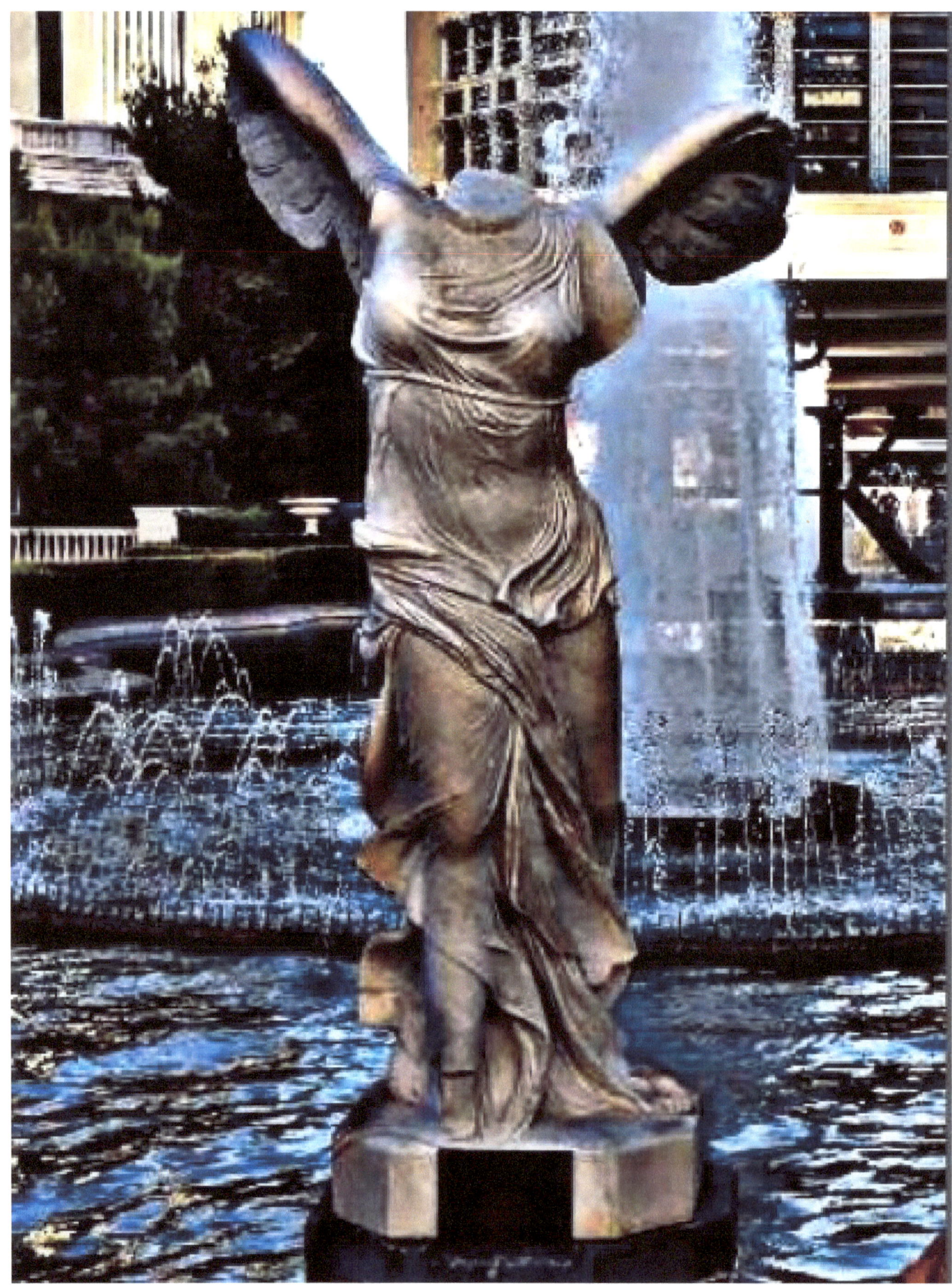

Headless Sculpture, untitled

Fave Art -16 (Funny and Sexy)

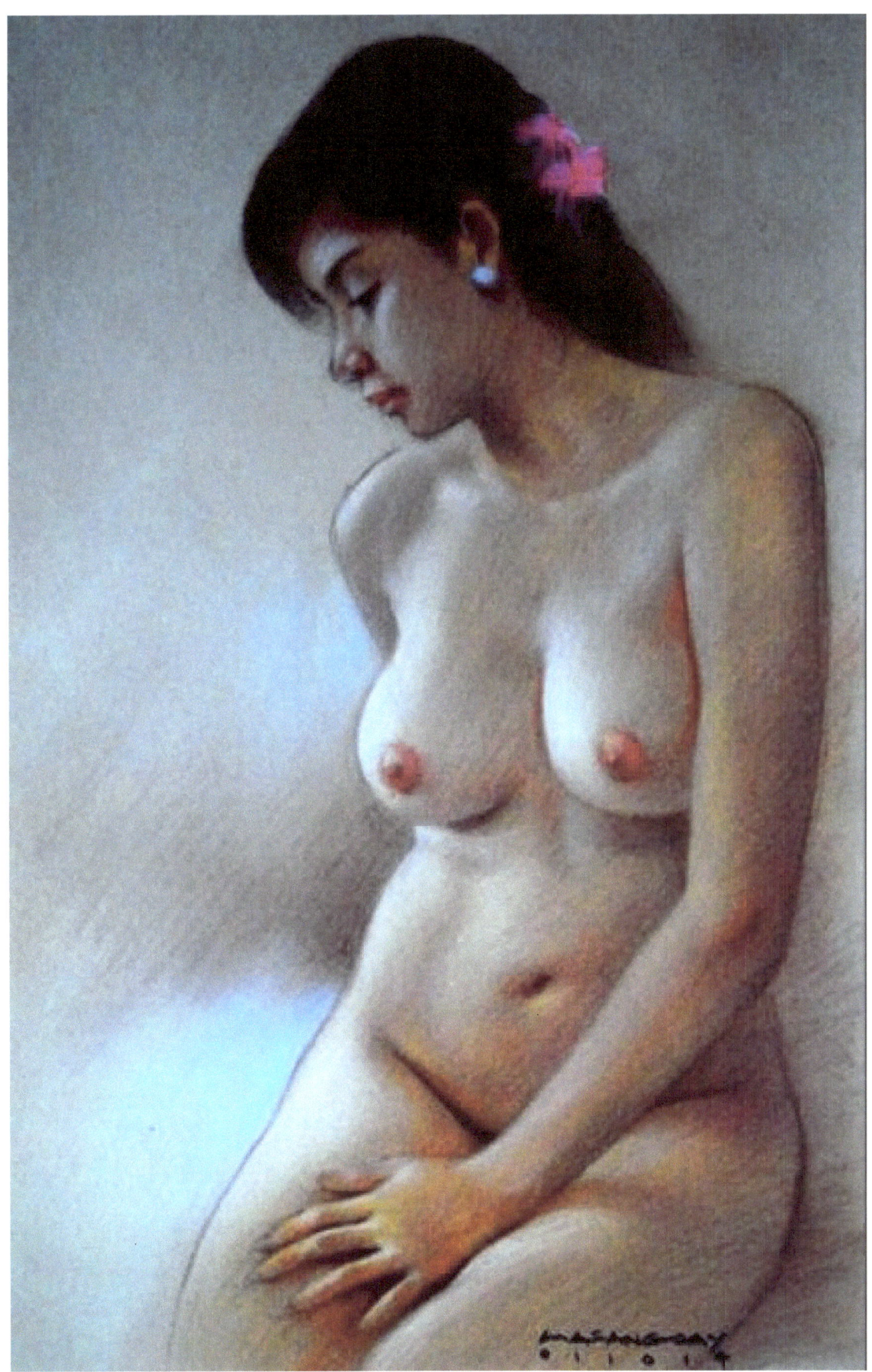

Nude by Nik Macatangay, a Filipino talented artist

Fave Art -16 (Funny and Sexy)

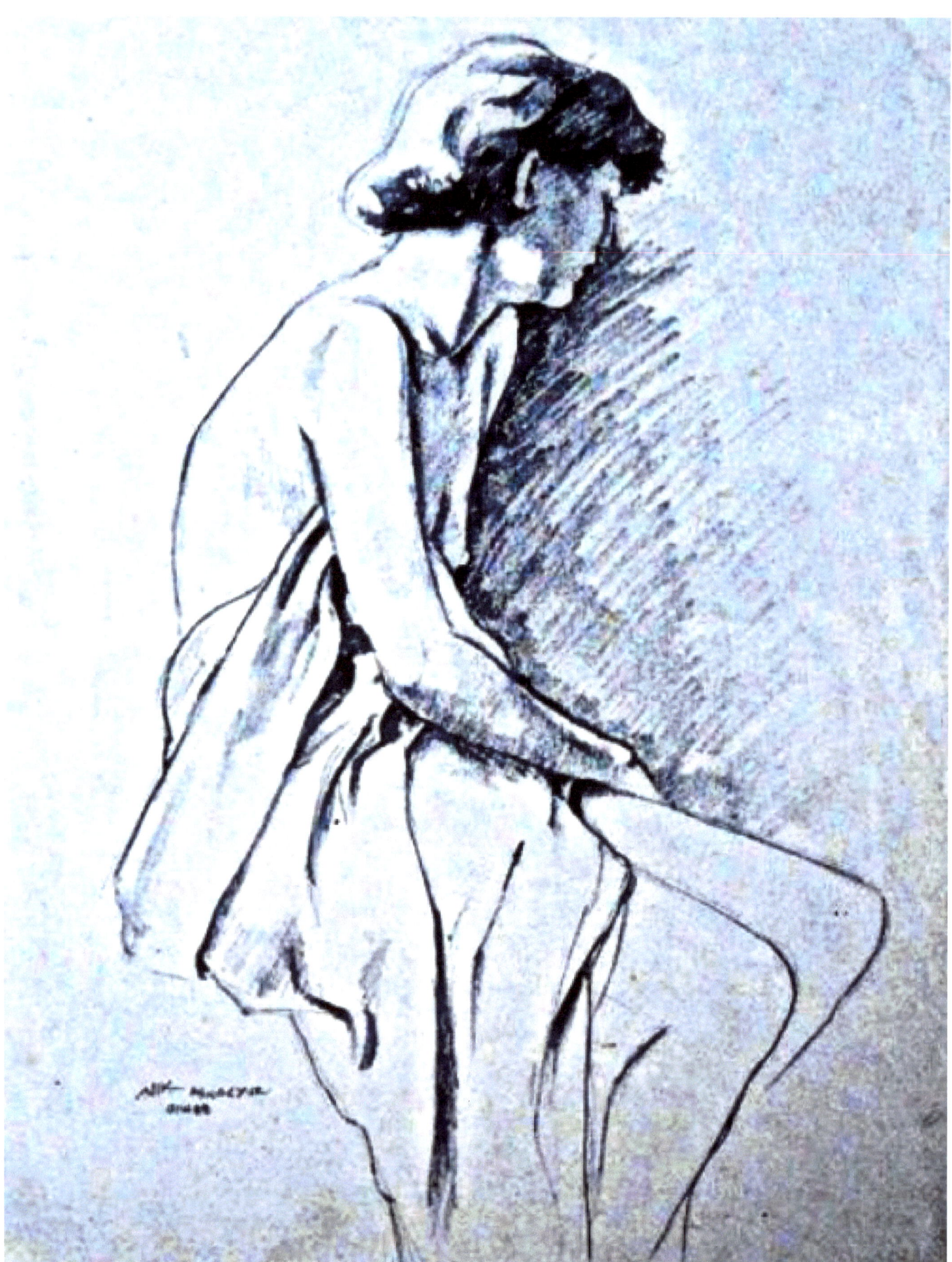

A Nik Masangcay artwork. He has a facebook account if interested.

Fave Art -16 (Funny and Sexy)

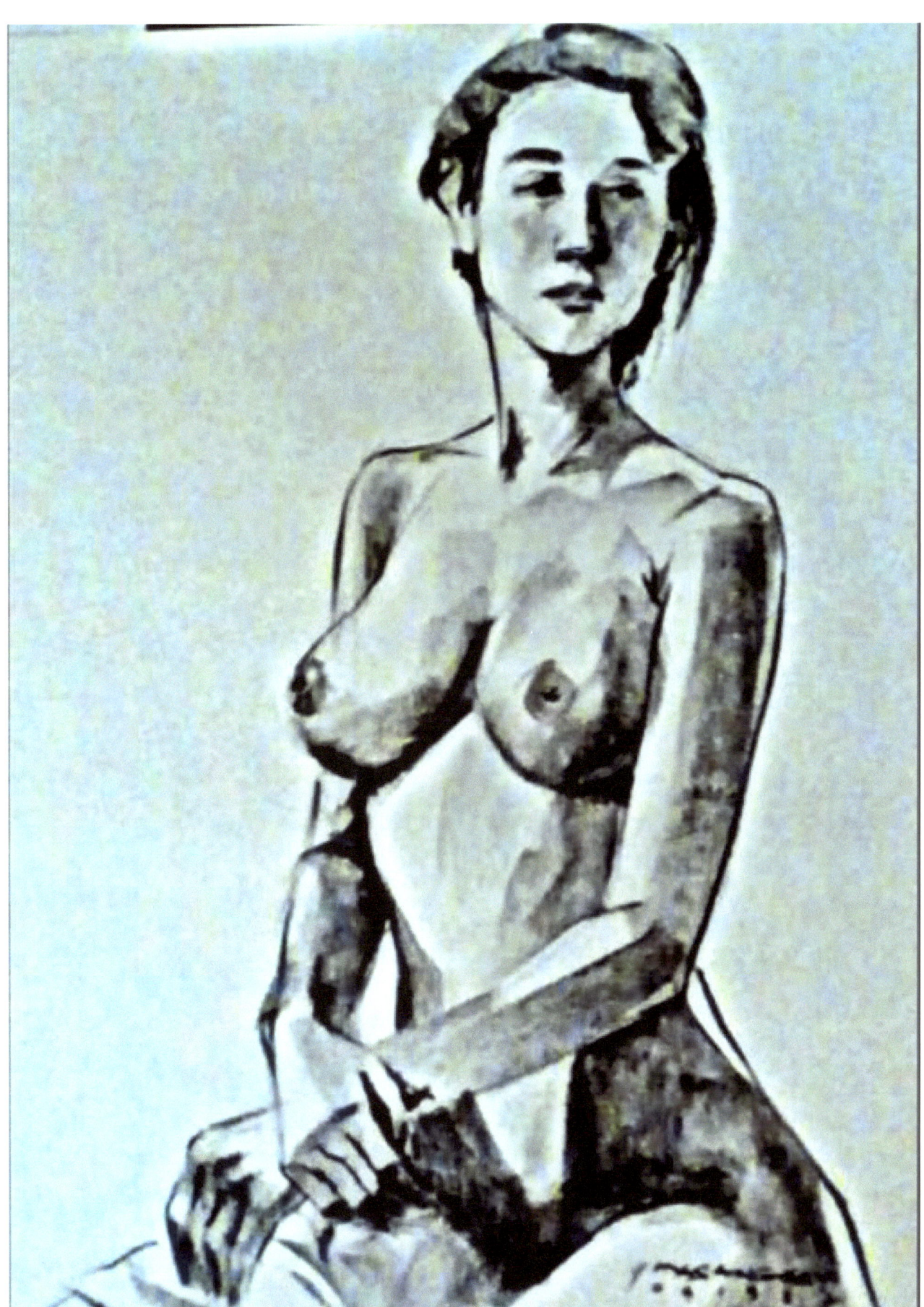

A Nik Masangcay masterpiece. He has a facebook account if interested.

Fave Art -16 (Funny and Sexy)

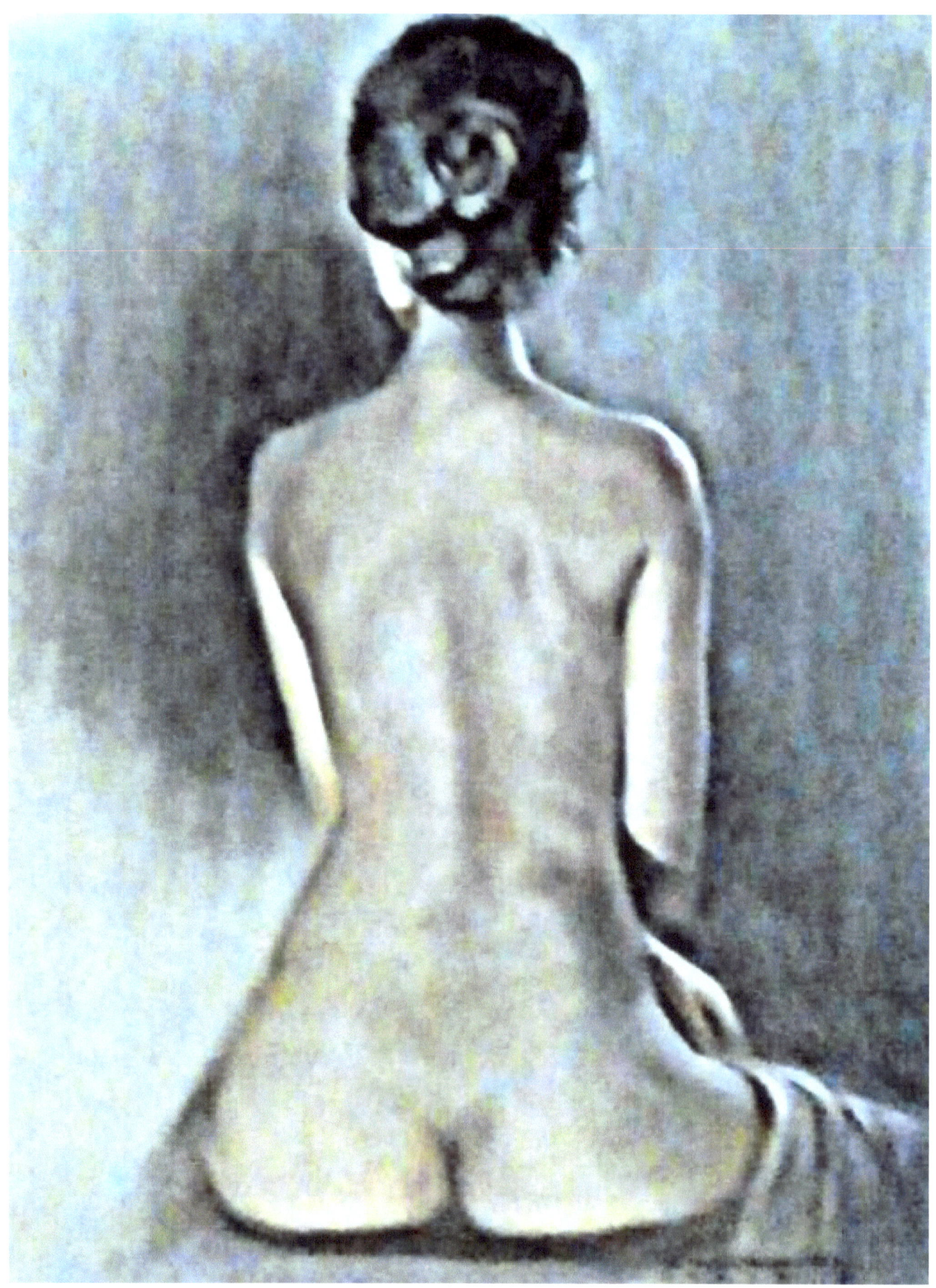

Another Nik Masangcay masterpiece

Fave Art -16 (Funny and Sexy)

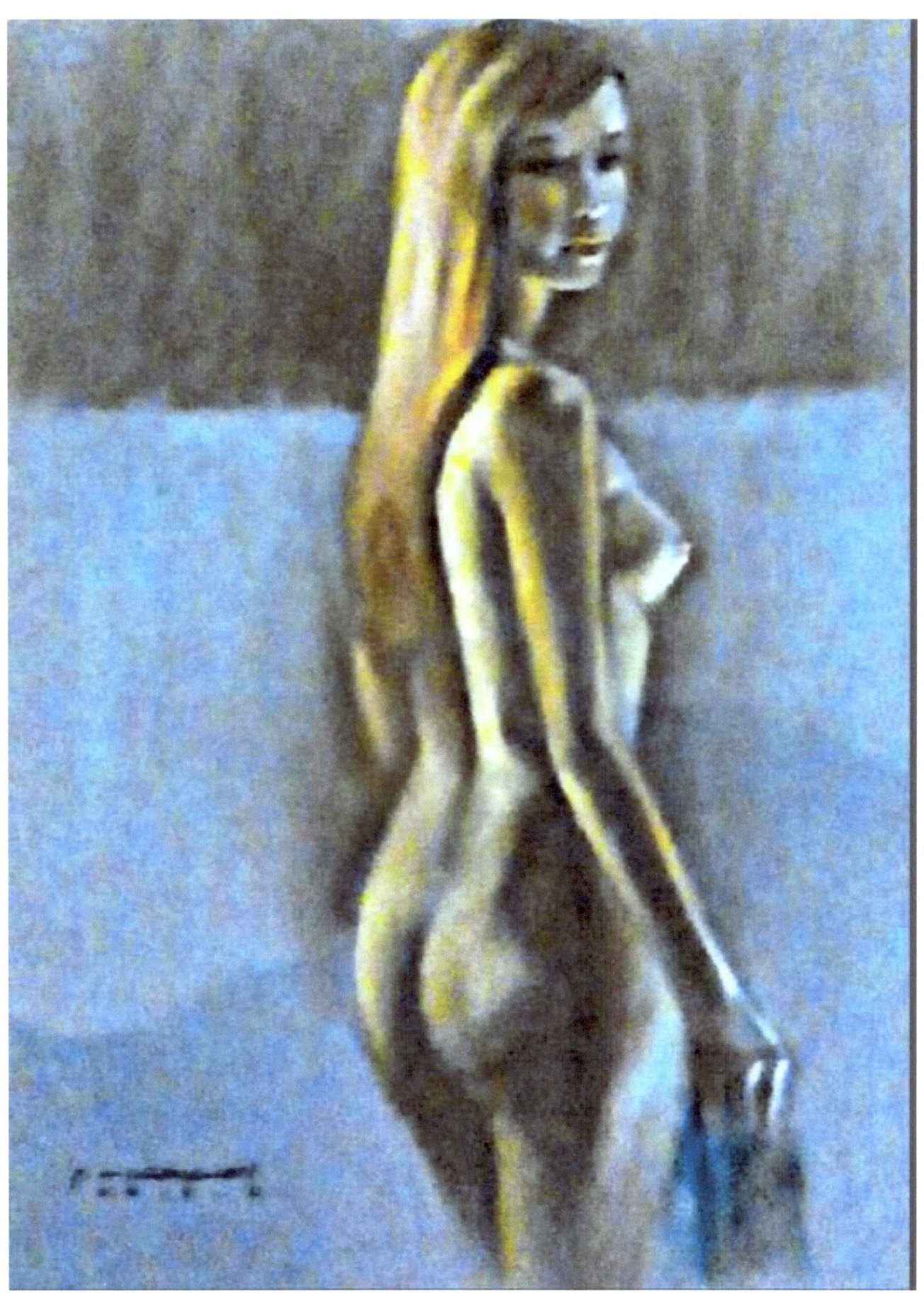

Another Nik Masangcay masterpiece

Fave Art -16 (Funny and Sexy)

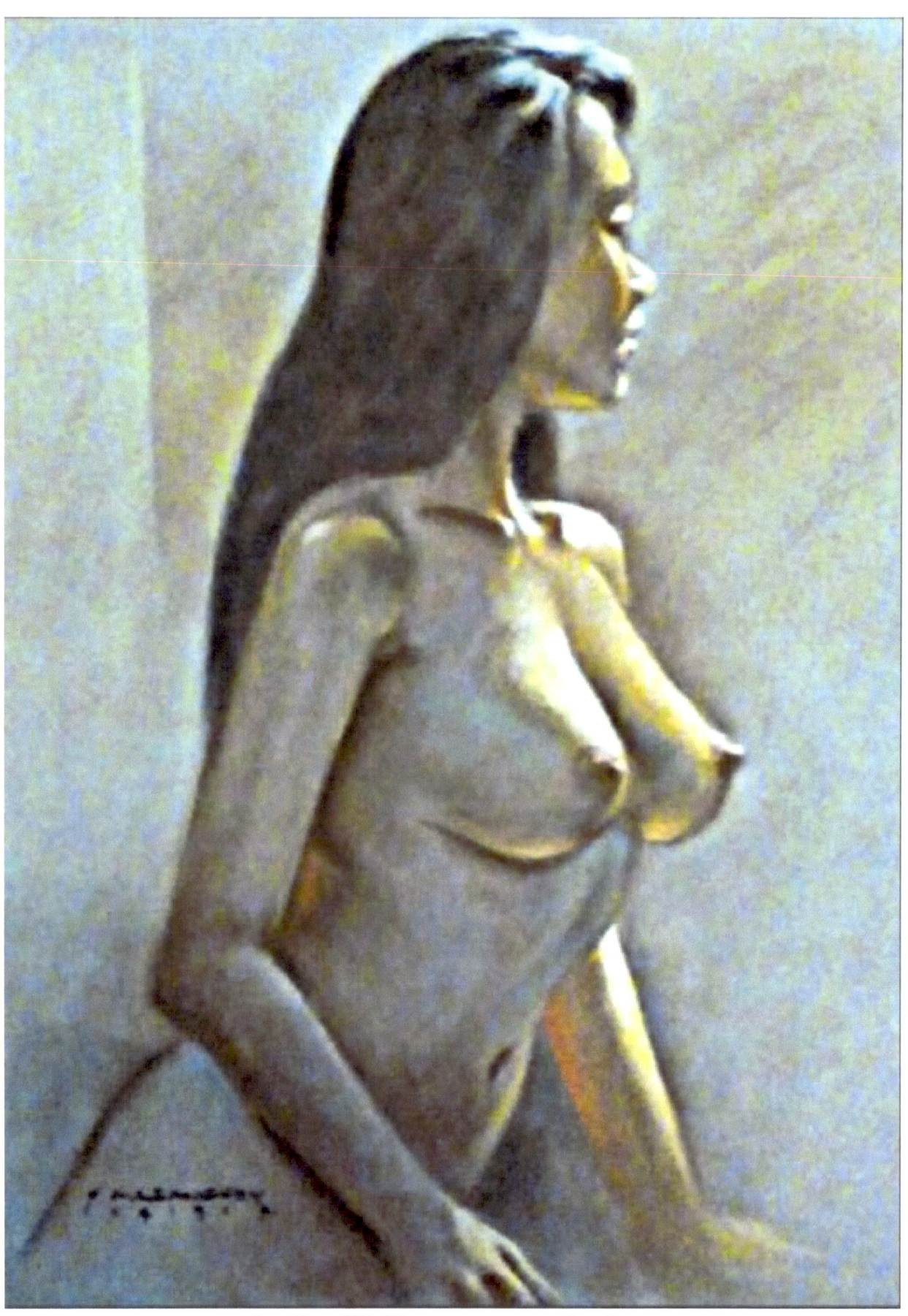

Another Nik Masangcay masterpiece

Fave Art -16 (Funny and Sexy)

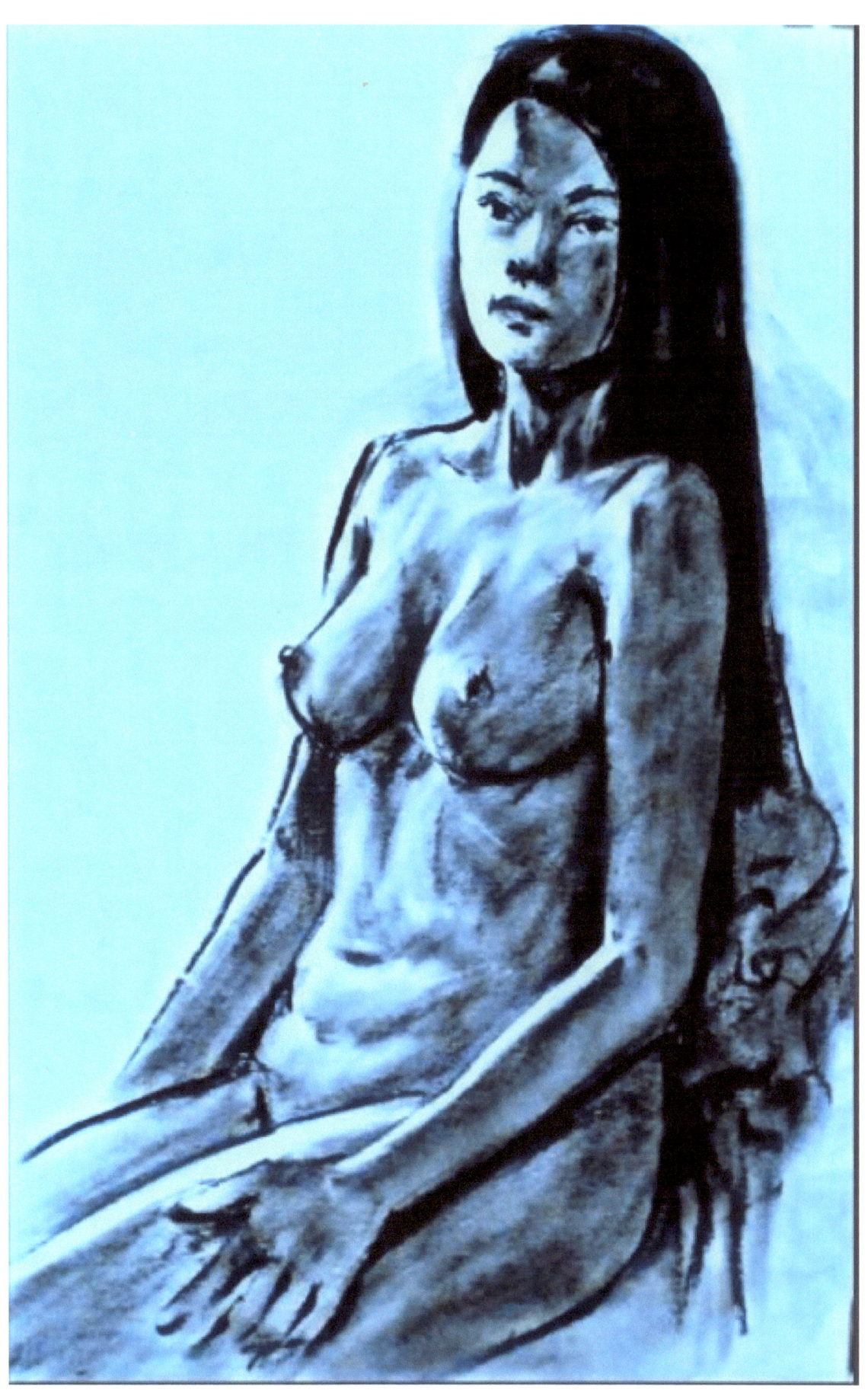

A Nik Masangcay masterpiece

Fave Art -16 (Funny and Sexy)

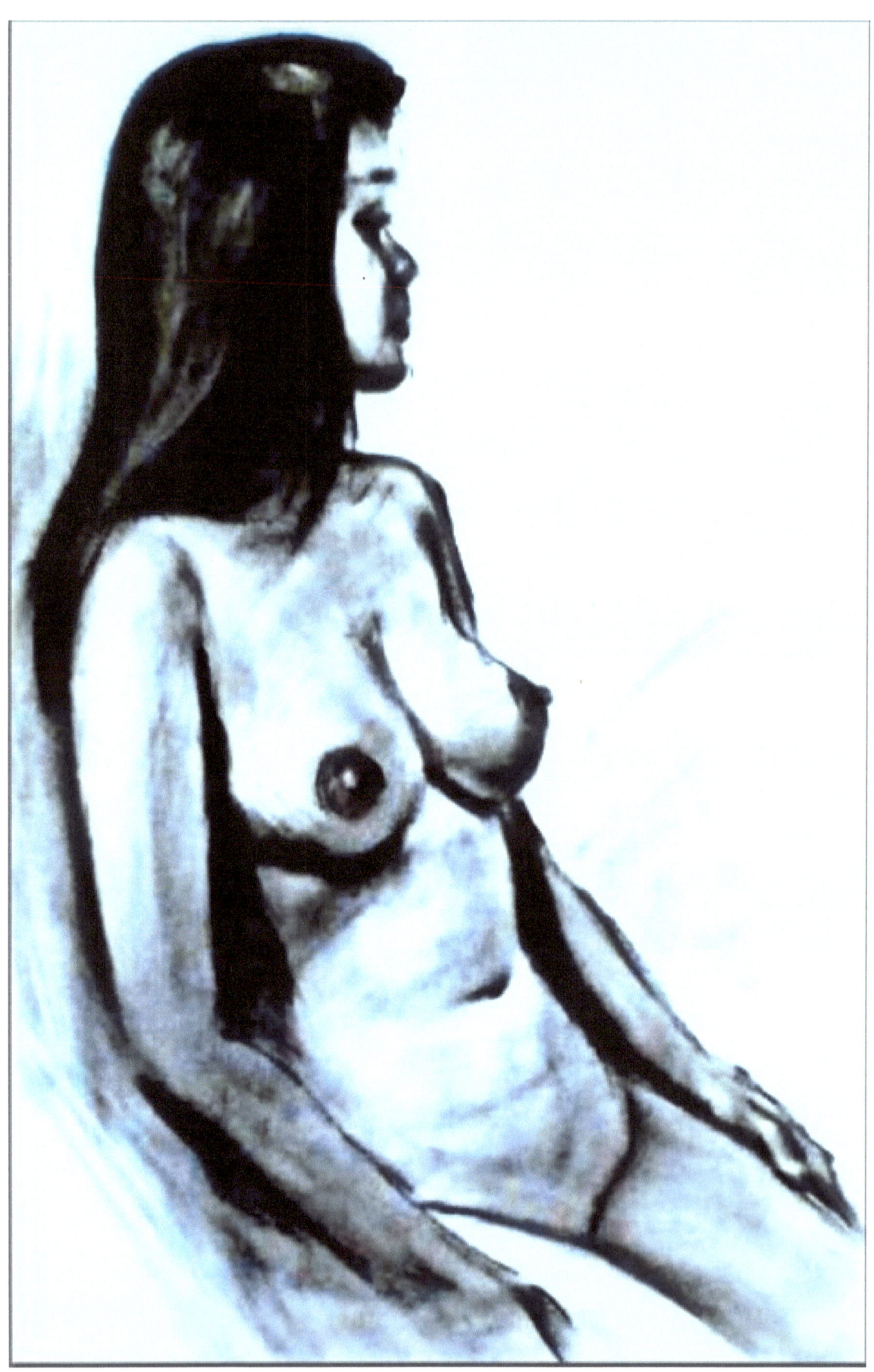

A Nik Masangcay masterpiece

Fave Art -16 (Funny and Sexy)

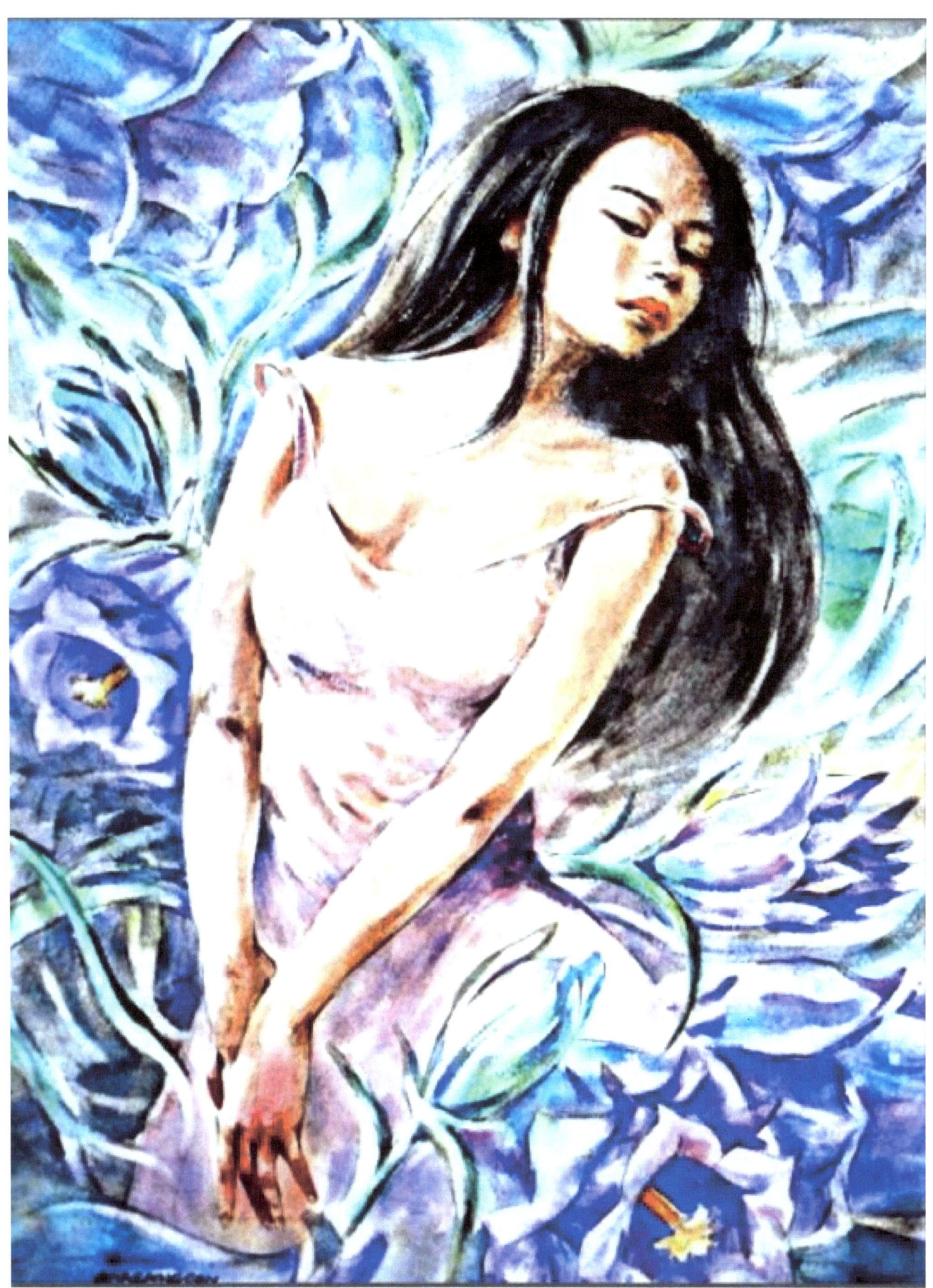

A Nic Masangcay masterpiece

Fave Art -16 (Funny and Sexy)

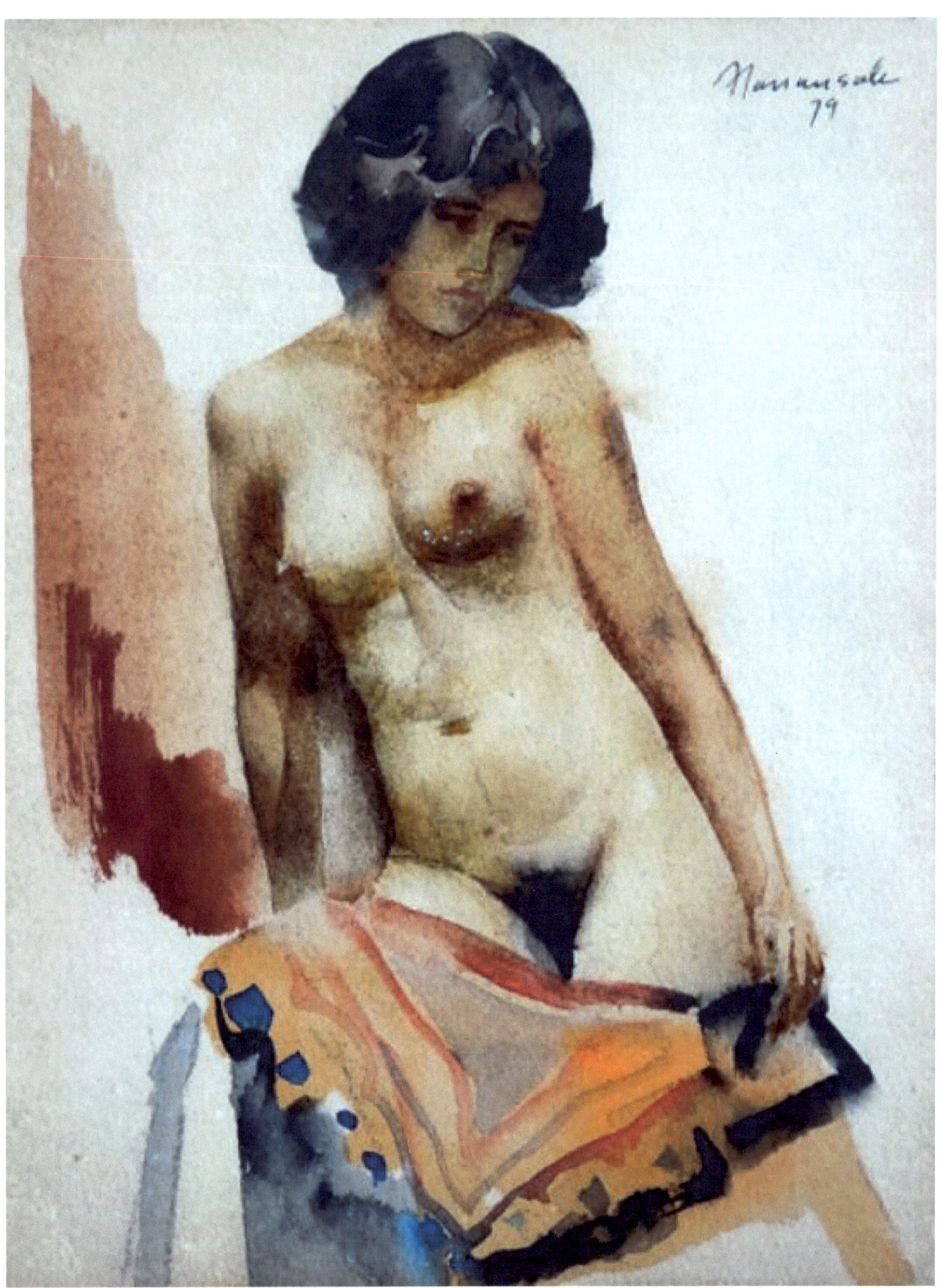

A Vicente Manansala masterpiece, 1979. He was awardee National Artist in Phils.

Fave Art -16 (Funny and Sexy)

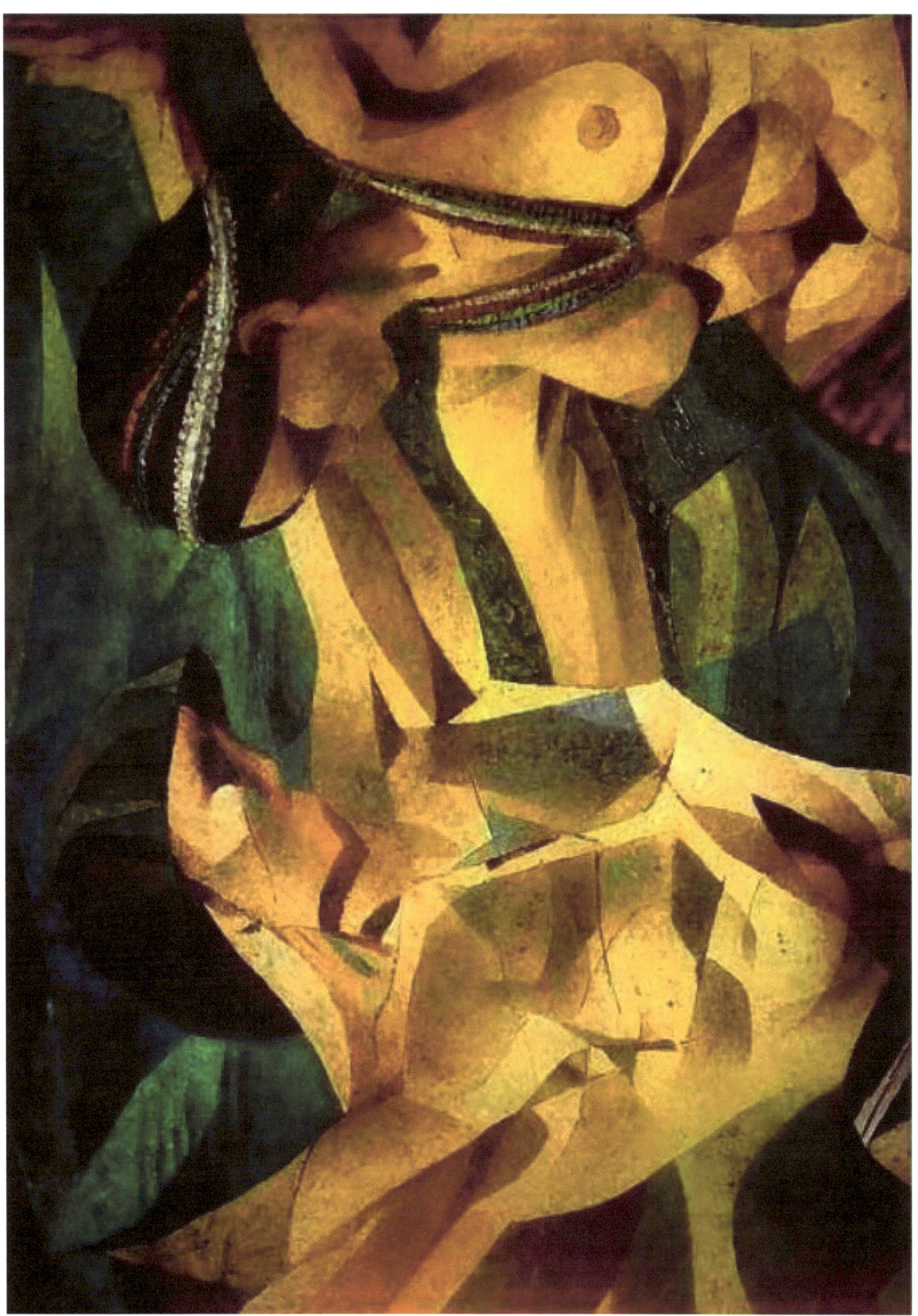

A masterpiece, Artist/Year unknown

Fave Art -16 (Funny and Sexy)

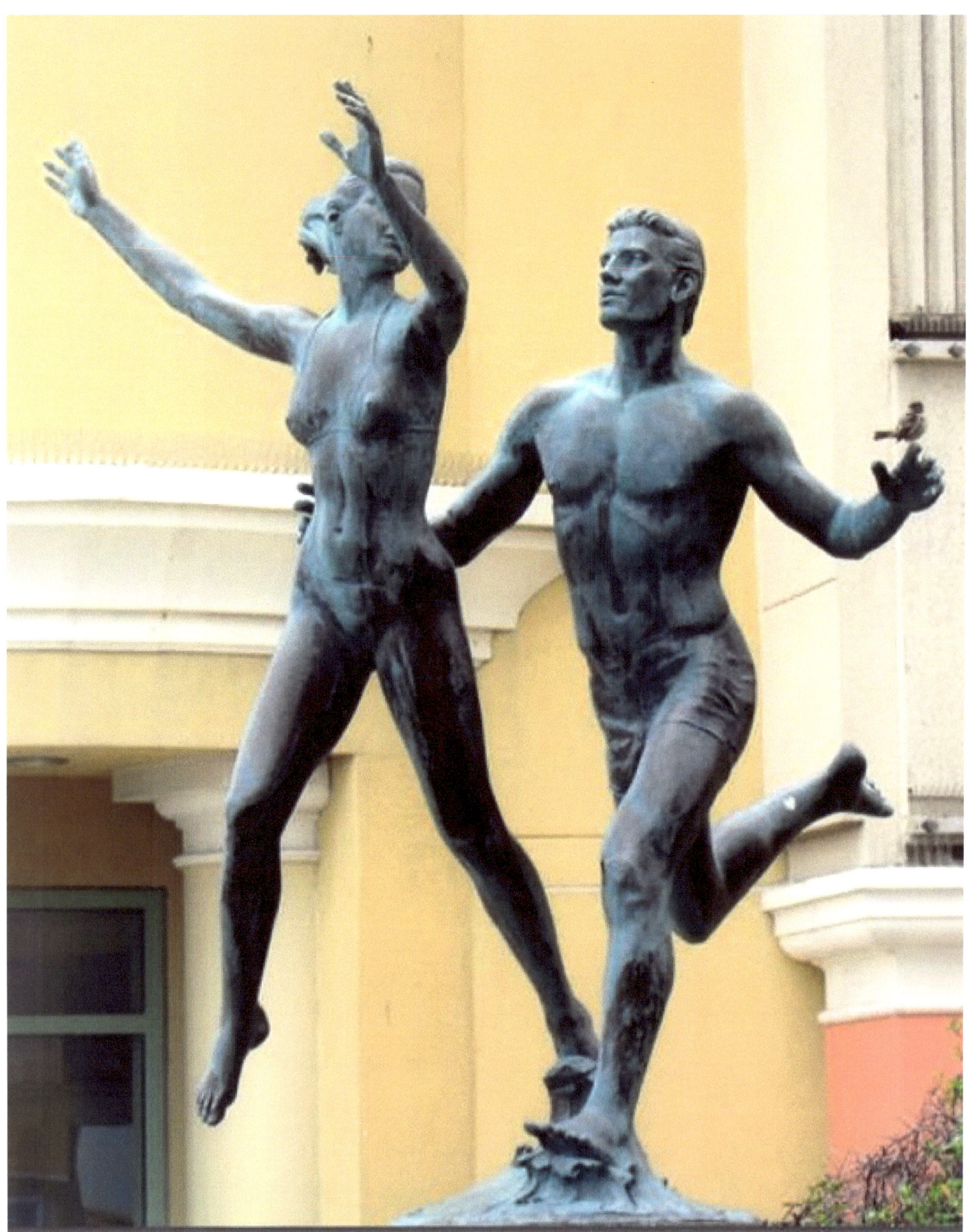

I took picture of this sculpture at boardwalk of Atlantic City, NJ

Fave Art -16 (Funny and Sexy)

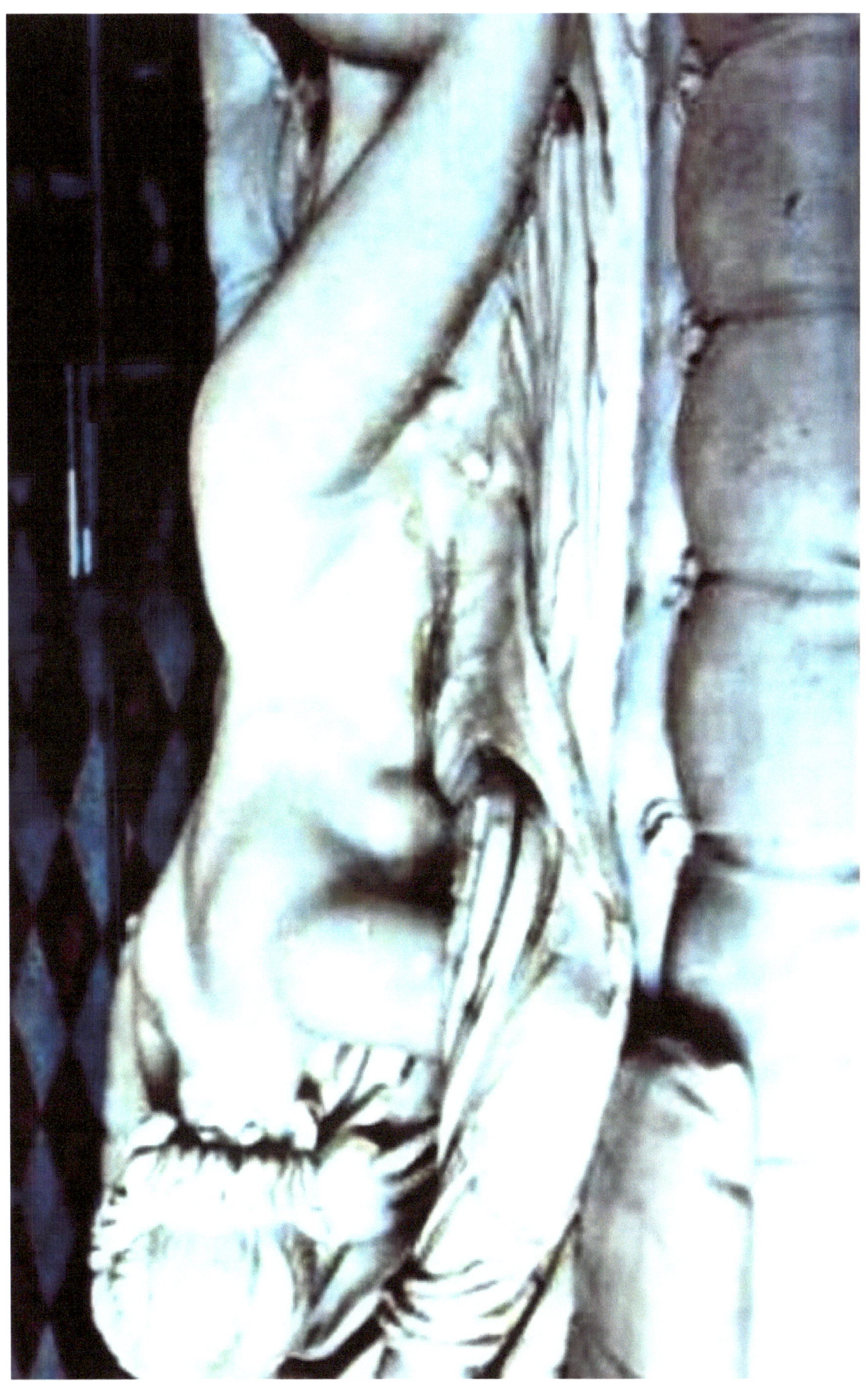

Sculpture lying down in a sidewalk in NY

Fave Art -16 (Funny and Sexy)

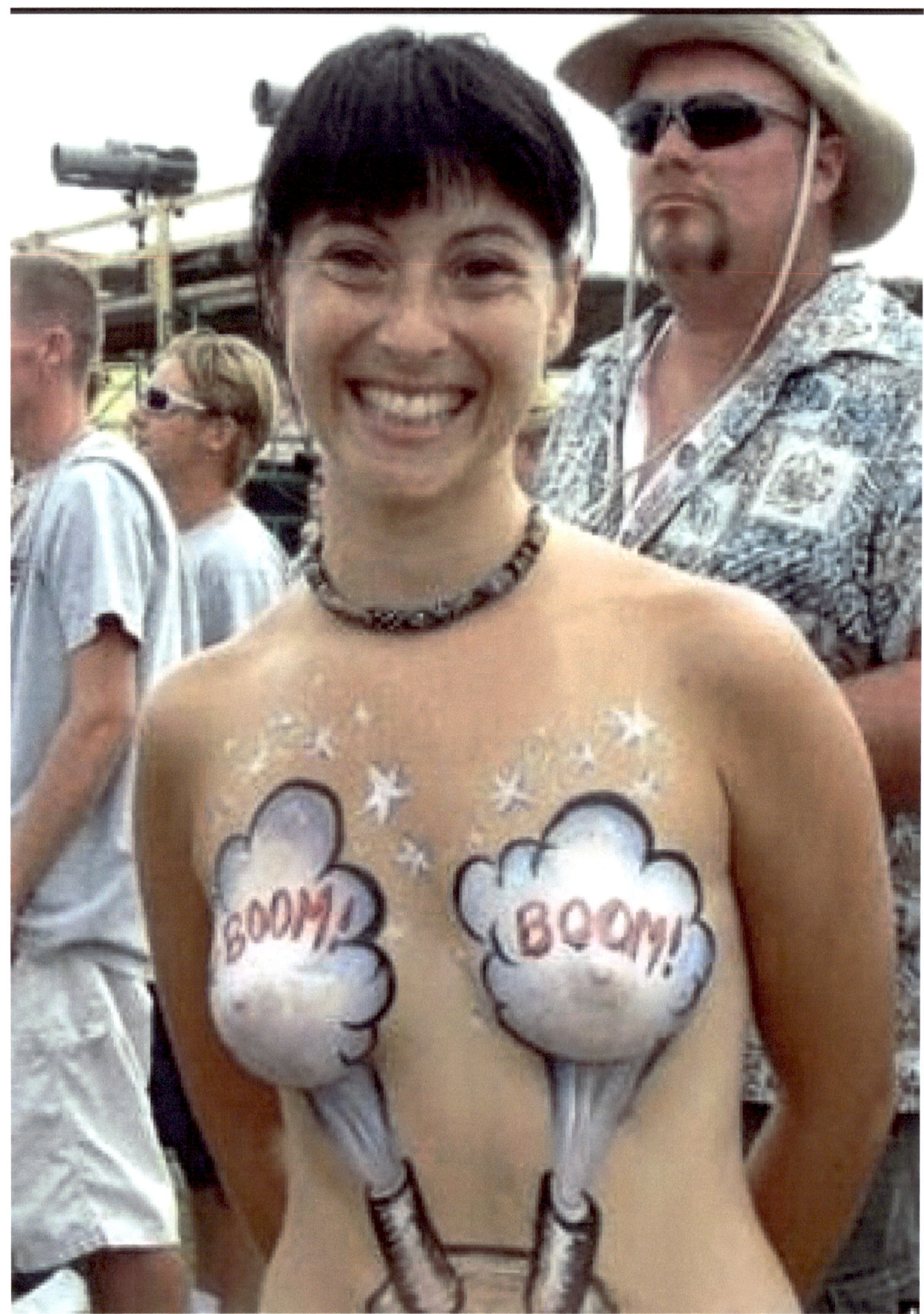

Two Big Guns – Body Painting

Fave Art -16 (Funny and Sexy)

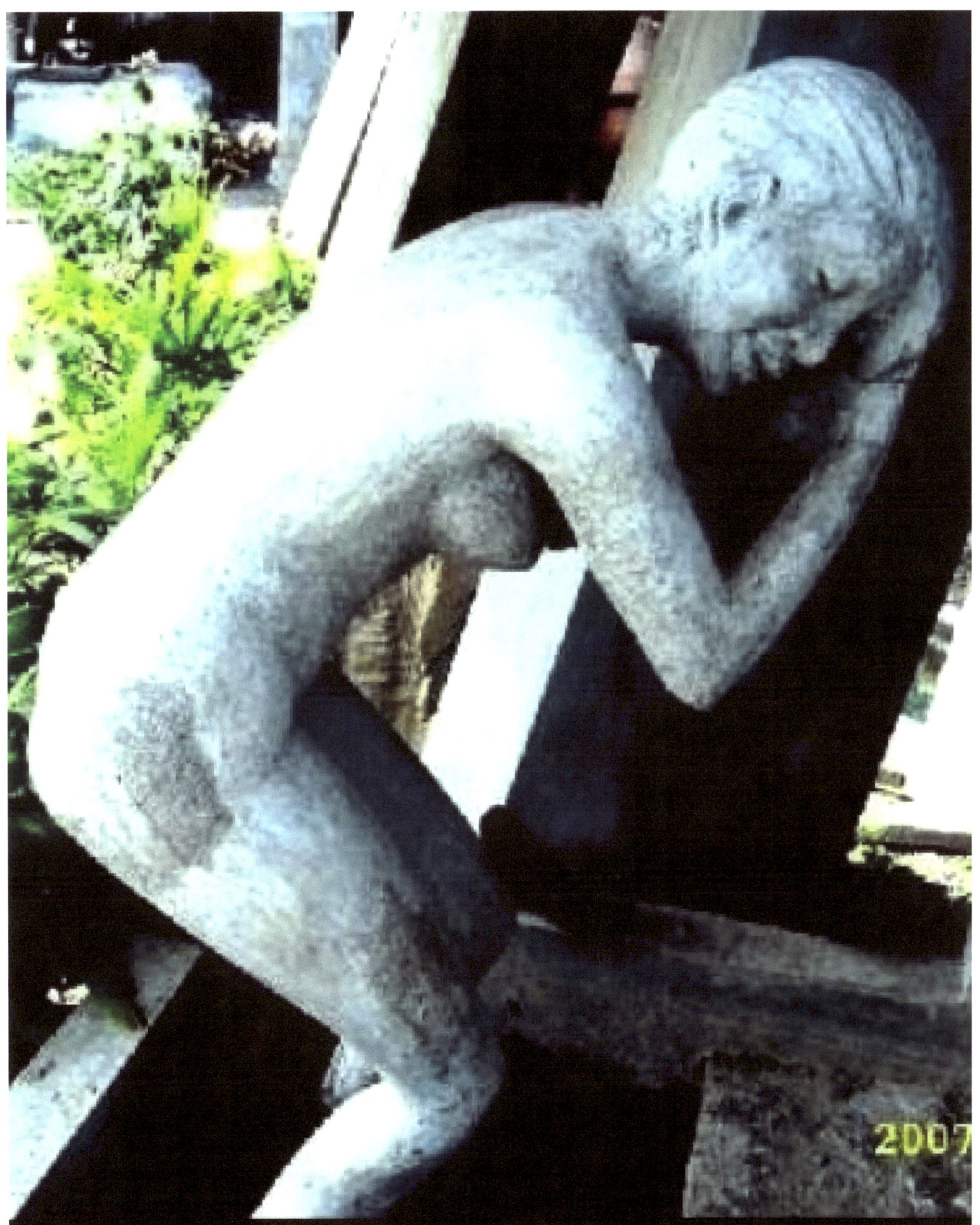

A Napoleon Abueva Sculpture

Fave Art -16 (Funny and Sexy)

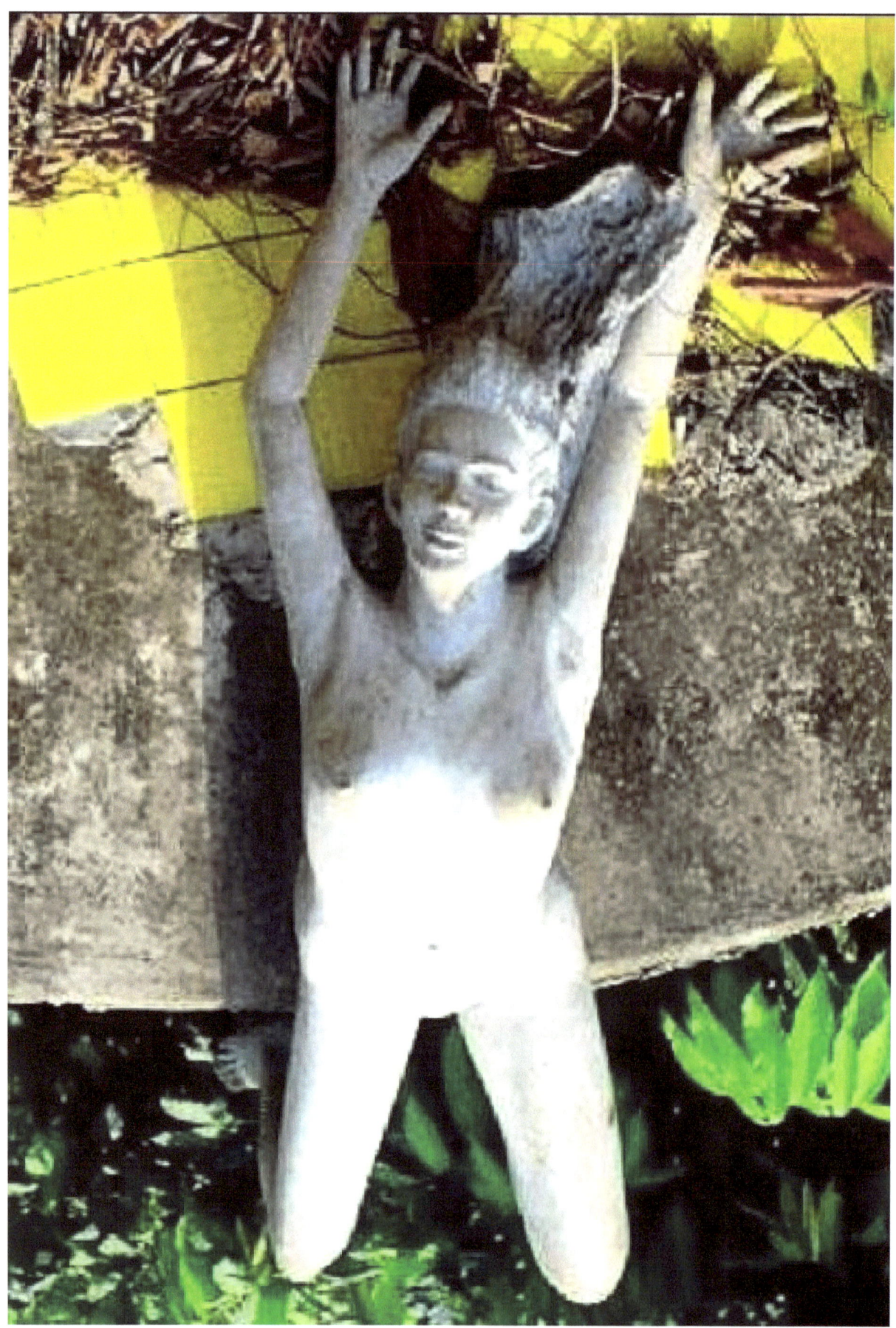

A Napoleon Abueva Sculpture

Fave Art -16 (Funny and Sexy)

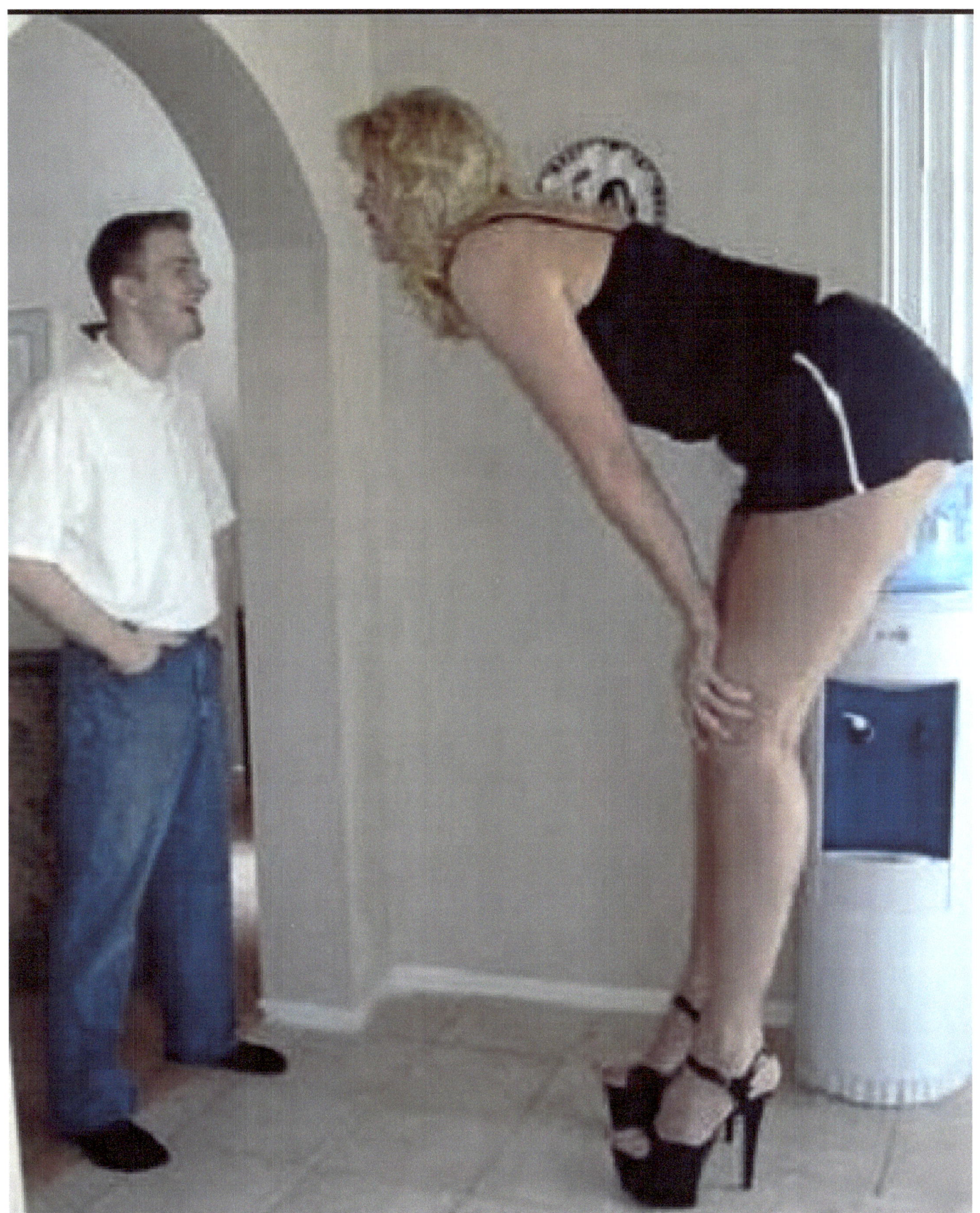

Big Girl

Fave Art -16 (Funny and Sexy)

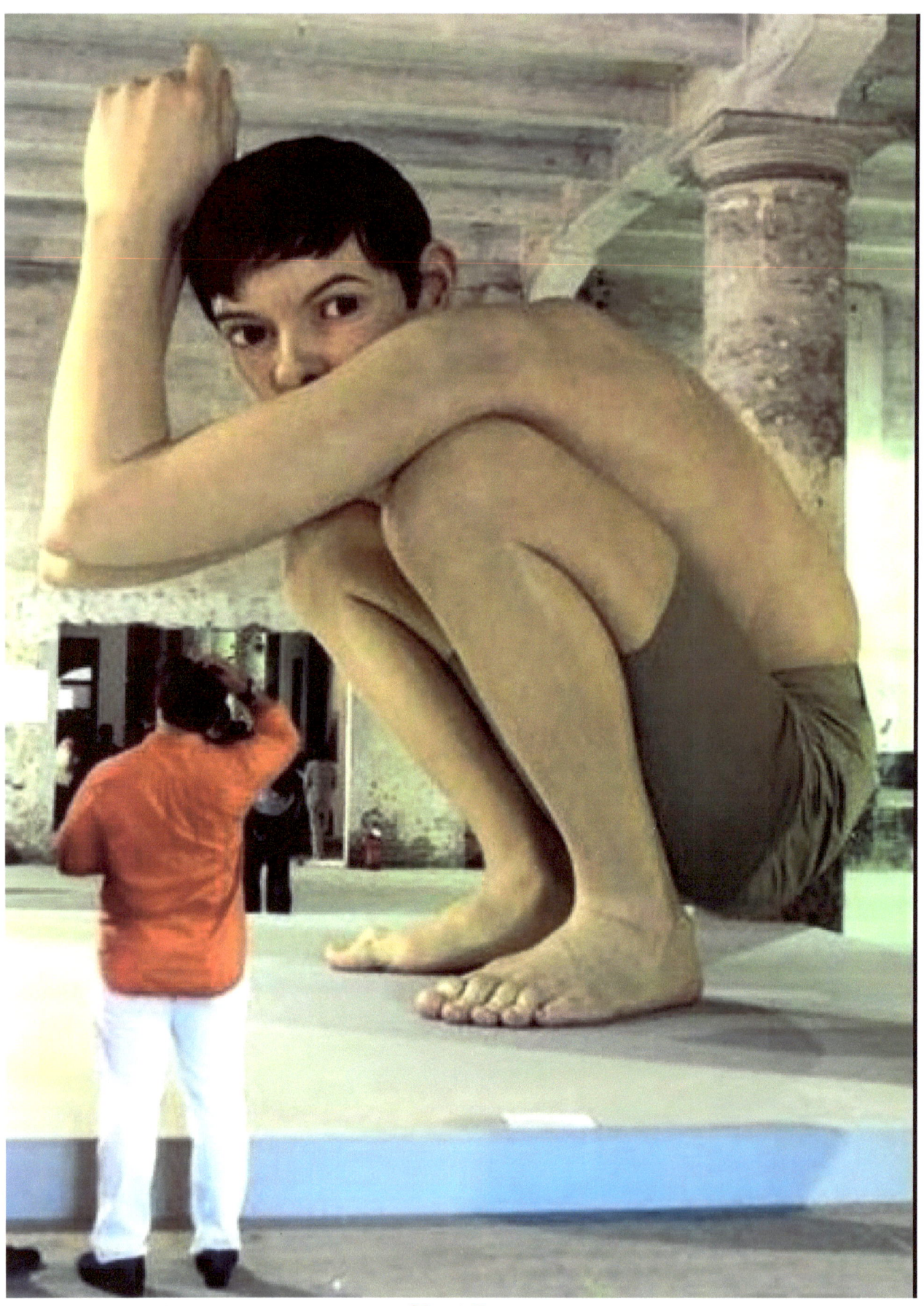

Giant Boy

Fave Art -16 (Funny and Sexy)

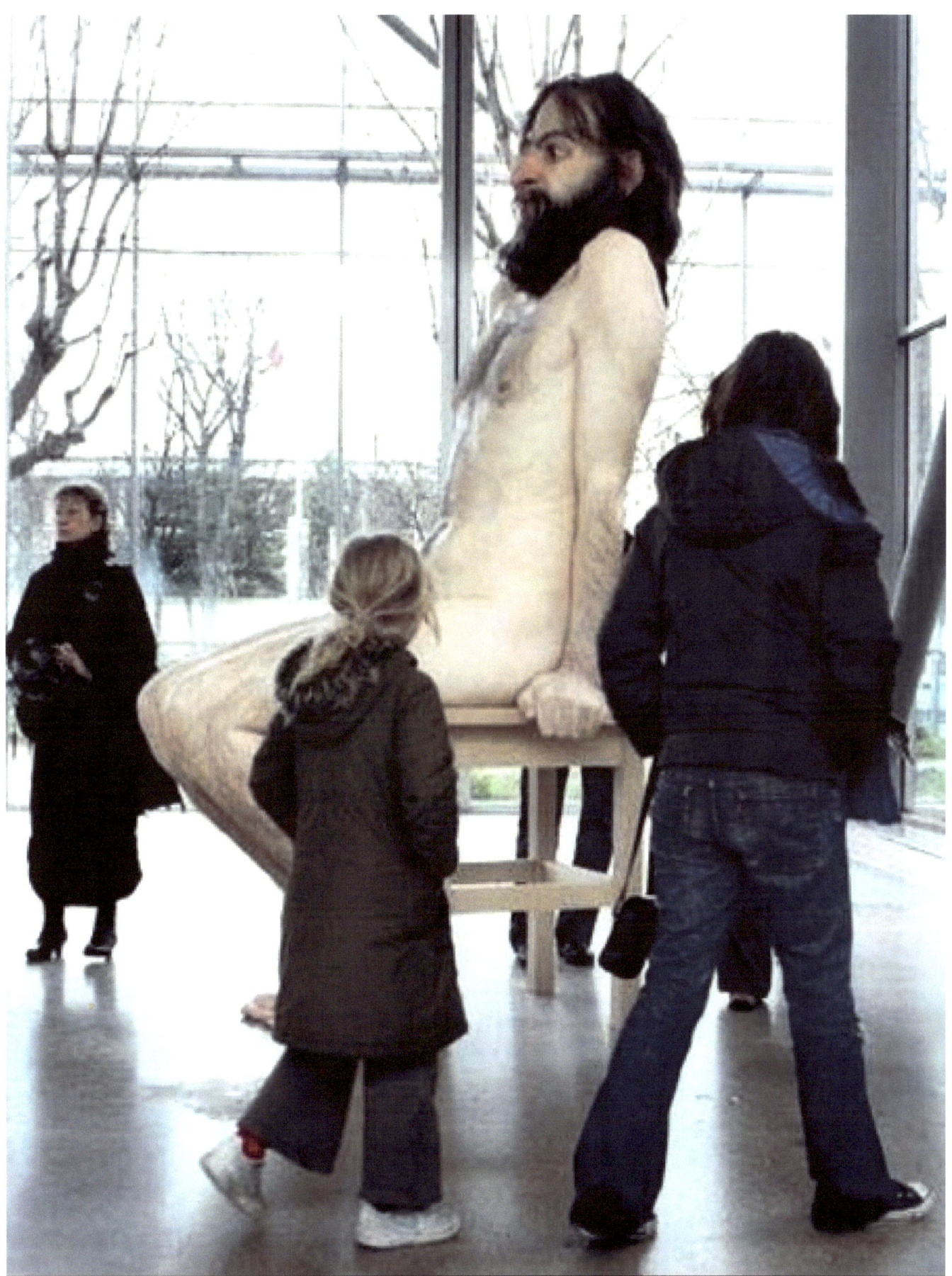

A Special Exhibit in New York by Australian Outfit (Looks Real)

Fave Art -16 (Funny and Sexy)

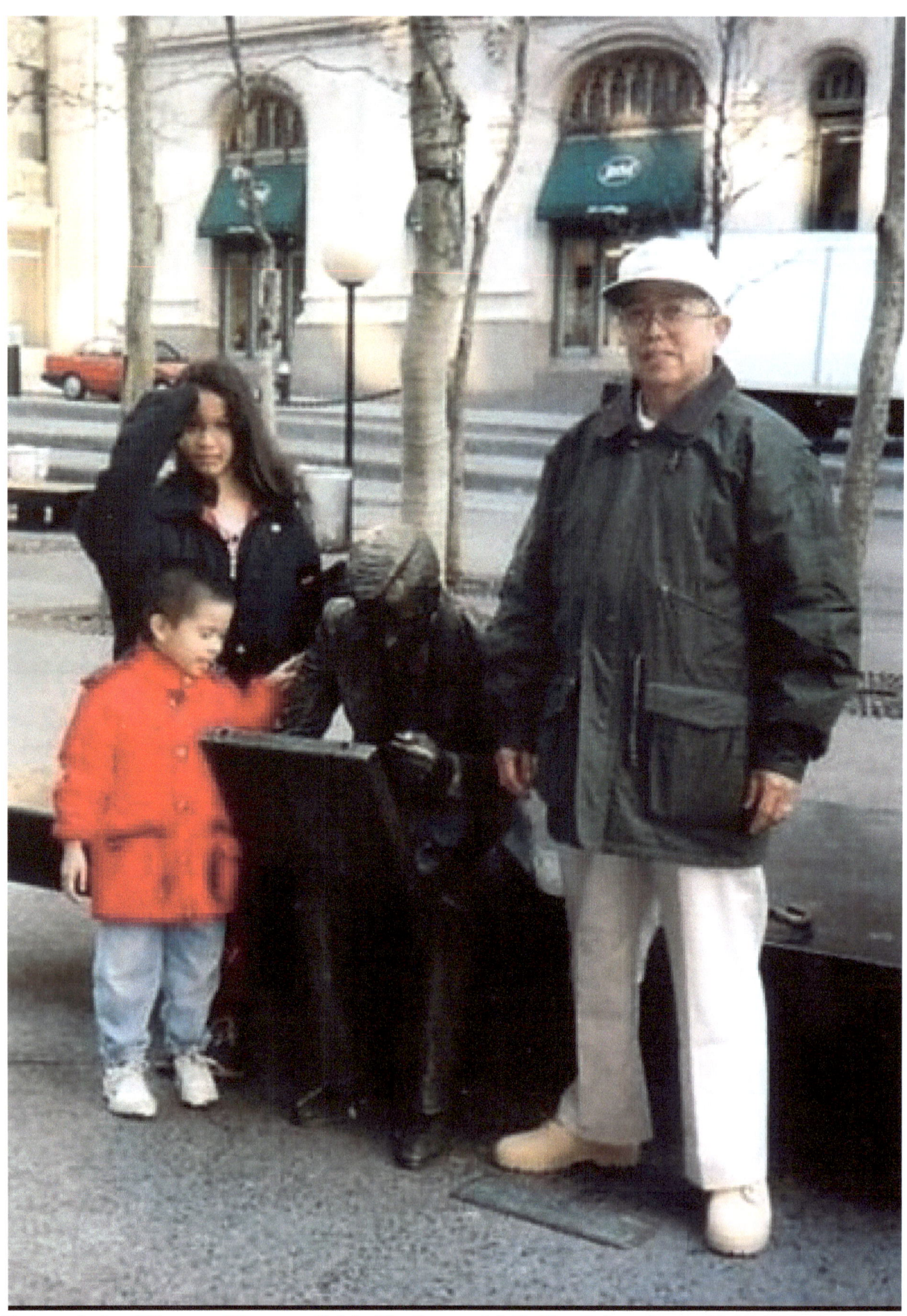

Tatay Jobo Elizes with grandkids Karines, 11 & Chad, 4 – circa 1995 NY. Taken at Ground Zero 6 years before 9/11 Disaster in 2011

Fave Art -16 (Funny and Sexy)

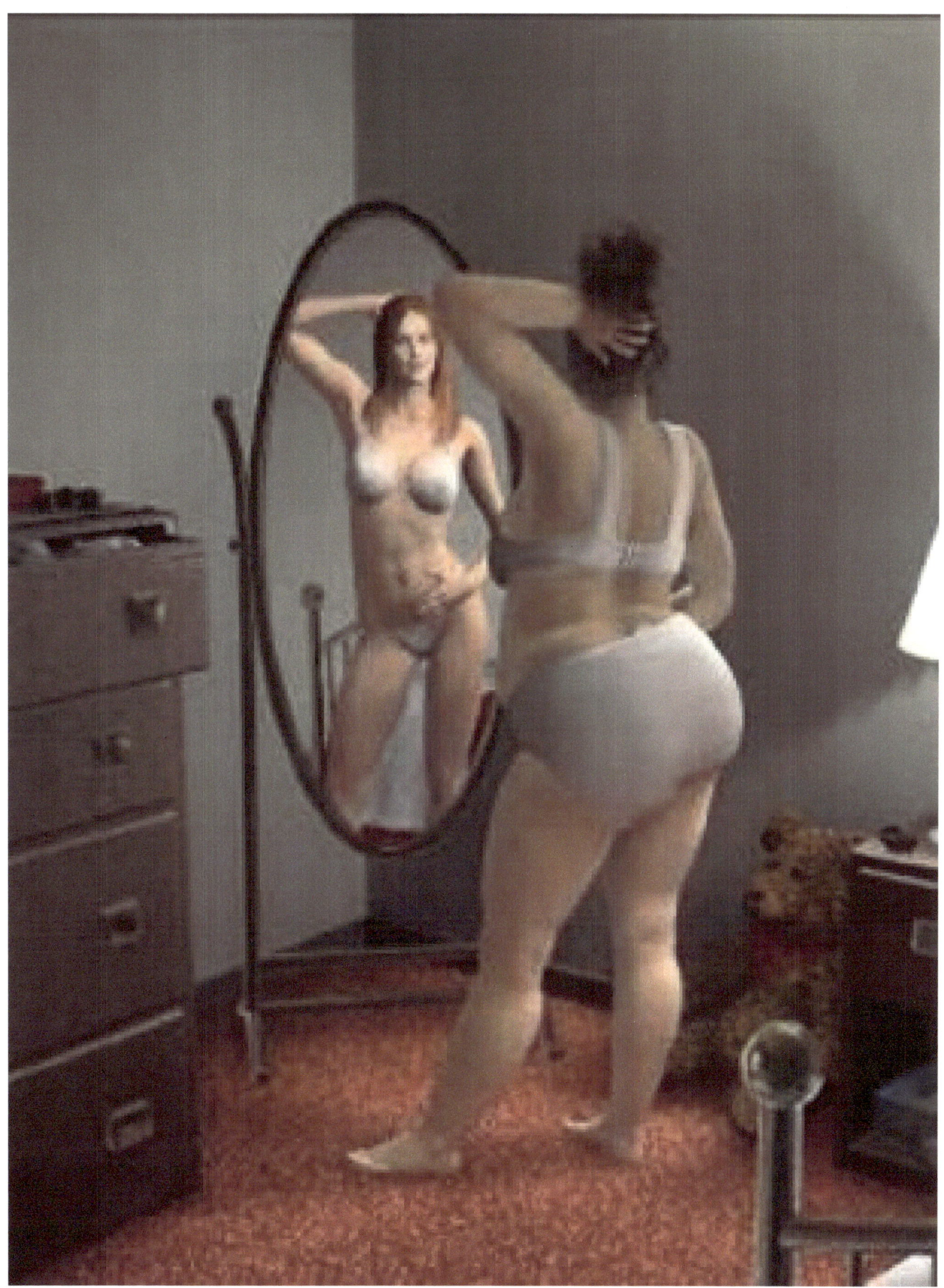

Optimism?

Fave Art -16 (Funny and Sexy)

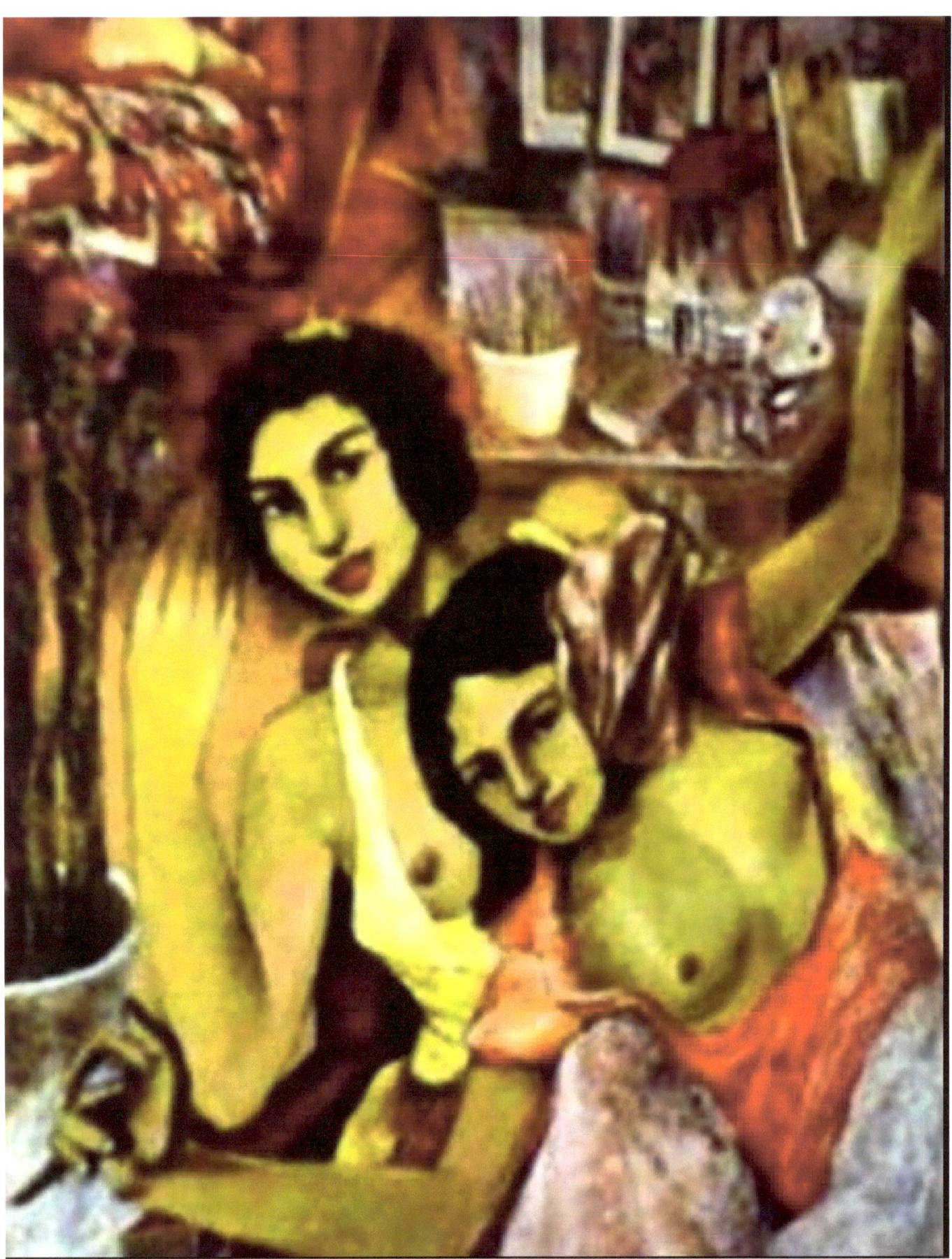

A Hermes Alegre Painting, a talented Filipino Painter

Fave Art -16 (Funny and Sexy)

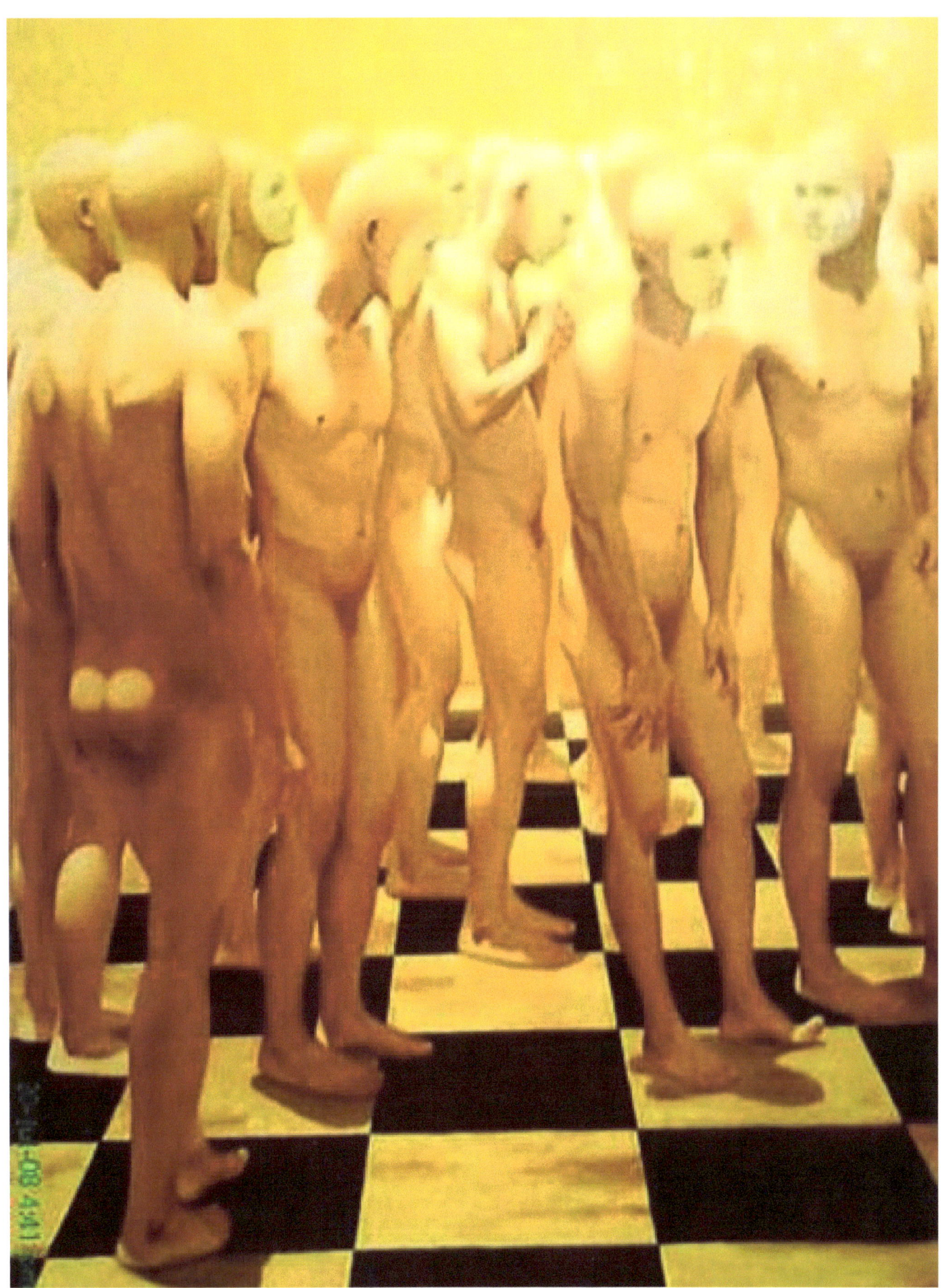

Incognito – Painter/Year Unknown

Fave Art -16 (Funny and Sexy)

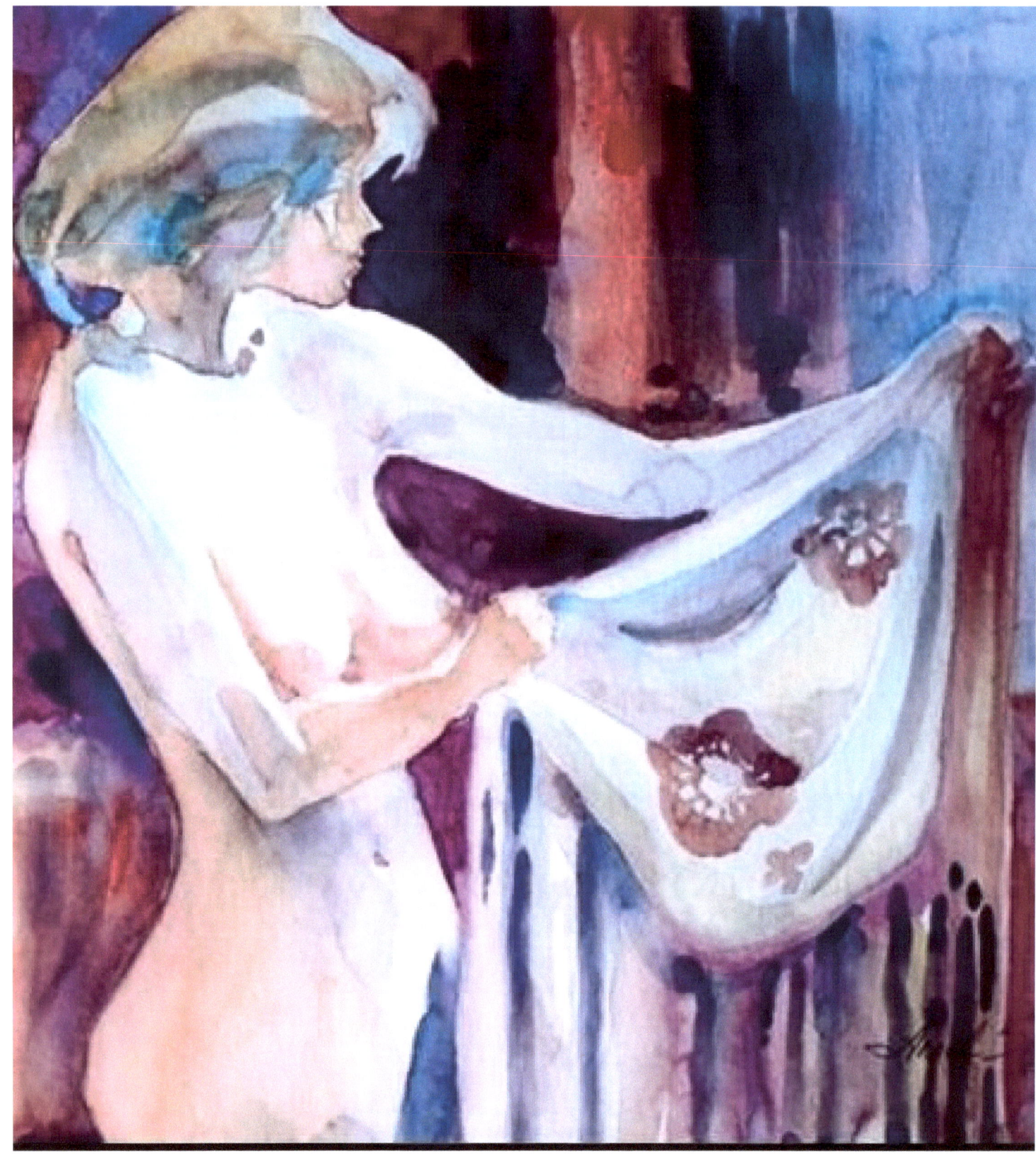

Trying a new dress – Painter/Year Unknown (illegible)

Fave Art -16 (Funny and Sexy)

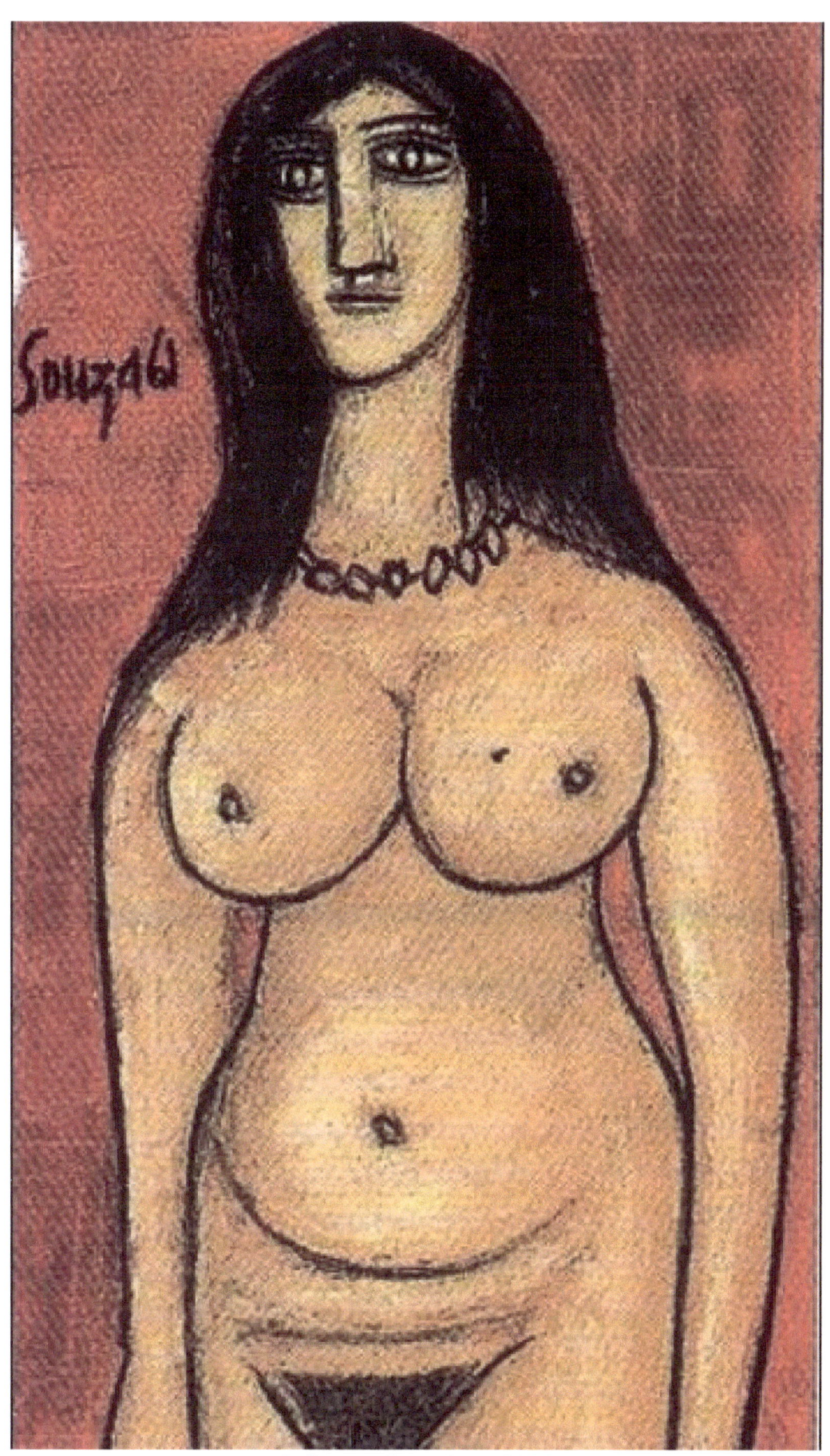

A Souza Painting, 1961

Fave Art -16 (Funny and Sexy)

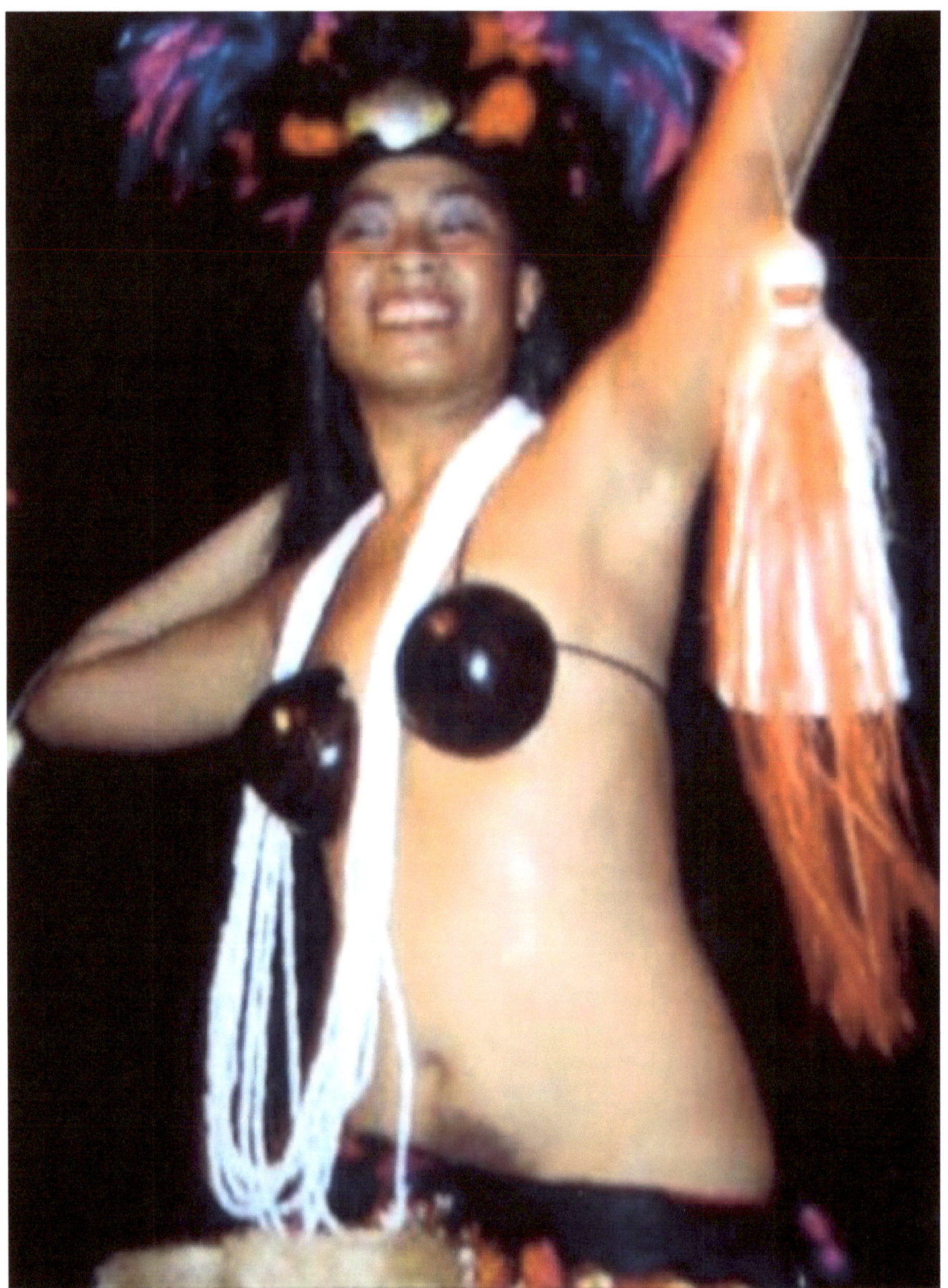

Hula Girl, Hawaii